Taking It to Our Knees

Rigorous Prayers for Life's Greatest Challenges

By Craig D. Lounsbrough

For information, or to order additional copies, please contact:

Beacon Publishing Group
P.O. Box 41573 Charleston, S.C. 29423
800.817.8480| beaconpublishinggroup.com

Publisher's catalog available by request.

ISBN-13: 978-1-961504-10-3

ISBN-10: 1-961504-10-3

Published in 2024. New York, NY 10001.

First Edition. Printed in the USA.

Additional Books by Craig D. Lounsbrough

with Beacon Publishing Group

Licensed Professional Counselor,
Certified Professional Life Coach,
Ordained Minister, Published Author

Join Craig at:

YouTube @craiglounsbrough
www.facebook.com/craiglpc
www.linkedin.com/in/craiglpc/
www.craiglpc.com

Dedication

I sat across from Charles, Madeline, Gabriela, and Eliana at a family barbecue. All were under six years of age. All were young, brilliantly bright-eyed, filled with the energy of untainted lives, and brimming with all of the precious things that we tend to lose on the journey to adulthood.

Sitting across the table it struck me that these children will inherit the world that we are shaping at this very moment. The divisive battles in our culture, the rising global conflicts, the descending morality, an unchecked sense of entitlement and more are shaping a world of deep uncertainty for these four little lives that now sit across this table from me.

The challenges in our world today are bigger than any set of skills, resources, expertise, or accumulated collection of assets that I could ever hope to bring to those challenges.

The issues that plague us today are far bigger than the sum total of everything that I am or ever will be. It is God alone Who holds within Himself the resources and the power necessary to turn the world up and away from that which is destroying it. He is our hope. Our confidence. Our single and sole light in a descending darkness. And as such I am forced to my knees before this God, for I have no other alternative that is even remotely capable of altering the course of our world. Indeed, He is our only alternative, and I would wish it no other way.

Therefore, this book on prayer is dedicated to these four vibrant and beautiful lives. It is likewise dedicated to the many lives just like them who are living out uncertain childhoods around this darkening globe of ours. It is dedicated to the goal of transforming our world through the power and the privilege of prayer so that their world will be what this one is not.

May the prayers of those who have gone before you leave you a world better than what was set before us when we sat at tables much like this one. And may those prayers envelope the whole of your future with everything that God would have for you, and nothing that He would not.

Thank you for your beautiful faces and the inspiration that I found in them on that day at that precious table. May each of you always remain brilliantly bright-eyed, always filled with the energy that makes you so very alive, always brimming with all of the precious things that make you who you are, and may you lose none of these things on your own journey to adulthood. May God bless each and every one of you for every day of your lives.

Taking It to Our Knees

Rigorous Prayers for Life's Greatest Challenges

Introduction

Most of my writing finds its root grounded in a passion for the subject about which I'm writing. There is something of a sustained and unexplainably resilient energy that remains consistent and reliable even when the demands of writing leave me spent.

But this book is different. The passion for which I long largely eluded me. It came as slightly brief snippets here and there throughout the writing of this book. But it remained elusive and largely absent. And my efforts to pray it into existence yielded nothing.

As I wrestled with the absence of passion and the question of whether its absence was a sign that this book was not to be, another thought took hold. The absence of passion meant I would have to press harder, dig deeper, and draw up a determination that would likely force me to a depth not necessarily reflected in my previous writing endeavors. It would demand a boldness, rawness, and a commitment that would challenge me to the best of myself and beyond. Maybe most of all, it forced me into a complete and utter reliance upon God, which I purport to embrace but often dilute with my own efforts.

It is then that I realized that such is the true challenge, nature, and privilege of great writing, particularly Godly writing. It shouldn't be easy, for then it would say very little. It should demand more of the author than it would ask of the reader, for how could anything less of the author be expected in order to do something more in and for the reader?

It would be fair to say that all of this left me with a significant degree of trepidation. I can't say that I wrote out of fear, for the very subject of this book would render such a statement as contradictory at best and hypocritical at worse. I suppose it was more of a challenge. A mountain to be ascended. A goal to which to rise. A threshold that I had skirted before but had eluded me. An endeavor that was less a partnership with God and more a reliance upon Him. Such was the writing of this book.

The topic of prayer is something that has been a part of my life for most of my life. However, it was largely piecemeal at best, pulled off some shelf during those times of stress or when the demands of life became too much. Prayer was an accessory whose use was limited to what I deemed convenient or necessary.

It was not until 2003 that prayer became something radically more. We have all experienced times in our lives when things in our world's collapse. And then there are times when the whole of our world's collapse. That was 2003. And in the midst of the carnage, I can distinctly recall driving south down a small stretch of freeway in Castle Rock, Colorado and suddenly deciding that my spiritual life would be decisively placed front-and-center. Not as some sort of lifeboat that I would discard once the smoke cleared and a new life rose from the ashes. Not some momentary salve to soothe the pain, or quell the panic, or sort out the chaos. No. This was a lifestyle choice. A forever change. A new departure entirely.

And this discipline became a passion. It moved from what I was supposed to do to what I could not wait to do. It transformed from some sort of dry spiritual obligation to the lifeblood that breathed something ever-fresh into the demands of my life and the rigors of my day.

Because this has now been the case for two decades, I have been repeatedly encouraged to write a book on prayer. Yet, I rigorously fought against the idea simply because so many have written so much about the topic. I find it wasteful to spend precious time repeating what has been aptly said before, particularly when it has been said far better than I could say it.

But then an email came, as they often do. And in the body of two brief paragraphs, it was suggested that I make prayer starkly real for a generation that increasingly doubts its reality. To do that, I only have to glance across the floor of my office to the two sturdy sofas where tens of thousands of hurting people have found themselves sitting as they grapple with unimaginable pain. The sofas that sit across from me hold in their folds over thirty years of memories of abuse, addictions, divorce, suicides, untimely deaths, crushed self-esteems, children destroying their lives, and people attempting to figure out theirs. And the question posed to me in this email was simple. Stunningly simple. How do you apply prayer to these people and their pain?

And that is this book. Short and simple, yet complex and wonderful. How do you apply prayer to the harsh realities of this thing that we call life? As a counselor, life coach, author, and pastor, how do you apply real prayer to the very real pain that life in our culture and our world brings into our lives? And how do we do that not as some nice exercise or elaborate endeavor? How do we make it raw and real? How do we do it in a manner that actually changes things? That is the theme of this book.

It is my hope that prayer becomes more real than the reality of your pain, or your loss, or your confusion, or whatever it is that you are grappling with. May it commandeer every struggle and move you to a healing you thought impossible. That is the 'what' and the 'why' of this book. And if it achieves these goals, the efforts in writing it have been well spent.

Section One

Chapter 1

Reshaping Our Understanding of Prayer

"Prayer is the humble man laying prostrate
before an Infinite God. And although it may seem
utterly ludicrous, a man such as this is one of
the most powerful men that you will find
anywhere on the face of the earth."
~ Craig D. Lounsbrough

We all have some conceptualization of prayer. How that developed is different for each of us. However, it might have developed, that conceptualization shapes both our discipline of prayer, our habits around this discipline, as well as the degree of passion that we bring to that discipline.

What Prayer Has Become

It could be said that prayer has become something lackluster, outdated, rendered a formality rather than a reality, and frequently marginalized in today's Christian circles. Sure, on occasion we pray as some sort of tired ritual in a church service, or at a funeral in an attempt to say something nice at time when things are not nice. It's that obligatory thing that we create a place for when the occasion presents itself, but it's rarely that thing that we develop a passion for as each new day presents itself.

Or prayer is that thing that we ignore until we're unexpectedly served with divorce papers, or find out that the diagnosis is terminal, or realize that our job is going to fall victim to yet another merger, or we fallen back into our addiction yet again. Prayer turns God into some sort of first responder that we dial up when the world's on fire. And when it's not, we never pick up the phone.

Outdated and Antiquated

Through our own lack of understanding and discipline, we have granted prayer the characteristics associated with some antiquated religious monk stolen away in some secluded monastery off in the woods.

Prayer sits on the far fringes of life as some traditional nicety that we toy with when we're not wrestling with bigger things. It might serve a purpose in life's special moments or in the midst of life's most dire emergencies, but even then we're not all that confident that it actually brings anything to either. To varying degrees we've rendered prayer as culturally outdated, logistically outmoded, a backburner endeavor, and far too simplistic to grapple with the monumental realities that are part of living in the 21st century.

Prayer is that seemingly vague and mystical discipline that's so ethereal that we haven't been able to figure out how or where to grab hold of it in order to bring it to bear on our circumstances. Life's running way too fast, or way too hard, or way too hot for us to have any reasonable amount of time to master this discipline, much less spend any time in it. So we hurriedly gather up the lesser things that we've declared as the important things, and we head off on some mission that is doomed to everything except success.

The Power of Prayer Forfeited

Prayer is not the frontline stuff that we bring to the battles. It's the invincible first wave that we typically never assigned to any wave. It's the force that we absentmindedly forget to bring to the battle despite the fact that it is lethally designed to cut the enemy lines to pieces before any of us can even step out of the trenches. It's the thing that sets legions fleeing in fear, but it's the thing that we set off to the side. In essence, we have come to view it as limp, less than viable, and nice but ineffectual.

Jesus As Our Example

Prayer is the first thing that Jesus did before launching His ministry. The first thing. The fact is, He did it for forty straight days before He stepped onto the world stage. That's how He started. With a scant three years to complete this massive ministry, He took a precious forty days of that time to pray before doing anything. That was the way that He laid the foundation and launched the movement that would shift the entire weight of history itself. He prayed because He understood the immense power and the uncompromising necessity of this precious discipline.

And if that was His chosen modality to launch such a monumental cause, then I think we'd be wise to pay a bit of attention to that. In a world that discounts the spiritual disciplines as anemic, passive and antiquated, Jesus drew upon it as the essential thing without which His ministry could not proceed nor hope to succeed. And from those first forty days forward, He rigorously retained prayer as a central and indispensable part of His ministry right up to the day that He prayed to His Father in His last moments on the cross.

A Needed Reshaping

Therefore, I would be entirely remiss not to begin this book by reshaping our understanding of prayer. In taking on that endeavor, I may do nothing more than tweak your view a bit, or I might radically alter it altogether. I have no idea how this is going to play for you. However, I want us to be grounded in what prayer 'is' and decisively move away from what it is 'not.' I want us to abandon all lesser ideals and embrace prayer as the potent and indispensable power that handily moves everything that would dare to step in its path. I want us to engage this book understanding the indescribably immense power that we wield when we fall on our knees and lift our voices.

To achieve that endeavor we might begin by asking what prayer is, but also what it isn't. What is this phenomenal thing that we have been privileged to do? How have we diminished it by adding our own contrivances to it, or attempting to tame it so that it walks in-step with our anemic agendas, or secularizing it to make it more palatable to the masses? What is prayer, and what is it not?

The next two chapters will briefly take up this issue as a means of deliberately seizing your conceptualization of prayer, unashamedly stripping it of what it's not, and delivering into the heart of your prayer life a cleaner and more robust understanding of prayer is. By engaging in this brief but pointed renovation you will find the prayer journey in this book more enlivening and life-altering.

You will find a more detailed dialogue presented in the next two chapters. However, to set the stage for this renovation, I would have you consider the following:

- Prayer is courageously living out our faith in the real world. It is not some ascetic exercise carried out in some mystical nether world.
- Prayer is a natural connection to a marvelous God, not an academic pursuit.
- Prayer is the rawness of the soul connecting with the goodness of God, not an obligatory tip of the hat.
- Prayer is discovering what we were built for, instead of questioning if we should have been built at all.
- Prayer is the activity which before all other activities, movements, people's and nations will bend if we just bend our knees. It is not some anemic exercise helplessly held within the four walls within which it was prayed.
- Prayer is not a lifestyle that we learn. Rather, it is the life that we were born to live.
- Prayer is not a formula that we concoct, but an intimacy that we develop.
- Prayer is not the last resort. Rather, it is the first step that will never leave us facing a last resort.
- Prayer is not the thing that we squeeze into our day, but the thing that squeezes everything that would kill us out of our day.
- Prayer is not a discipline, but a manifestation of our love for our God that results in a discipline.
- Prayer is the choice to invade the impossible, not live out our lives hampered by the probable.

I would suggest that you take a few moments to ponder these points before moving on to the next chapter. I would let them begin the process of reshaping your understanding of prayer and the manner in which you will engage this incredible privilege from this moment forward.

Notes:

Section One

Chapter 2

What Prayer is Not

"If you've been foolish enough to underestimate the power of prayer then you've probably been naive enough to overestimate the power of everything else."

~ Craig D. Lounsbrough

Much of what makes up our prayers is what prayer is 'not,' making prayer what it is not. We would be hard pressed to admit that, but what we call 'prayer' is often something culturally diluted and intellectually parsed. We are left with something so altogether different in both form and power that we cannot cleanly fit it into any Biblical definition of prayer regardless of how hard we attempt to force-fit it.

Too often we have shaped prayer to our culture, and not our culture to prayer. We have set about to determine how prayer can be used as a tool in the process of achieving our goals, verses being a process where we determine what those goals should be. Prayer has become a largely abandoned stepchild to our selfishness, and it has been bent to irrelevance by our lackluster faith.

In essence, we have practiced prayer while destroying it in the practice of it. It's power and transformational essence have been unduly subjugated to a compromised belief system that has cut the legs out from under our faith. Such a destructive orientation has served to render our message one of obscurity and irrelevance.

In order to truly embrace prayer, we would be wise to determine what it is 'not.' Such an exercise is absolutely critical, despite how painful it might be. Too often, what prayer is 'not' has been so thoroughly (and convincingly) incorporated into our understanding of prayer that we've embraced what it is 'not' as being what it 'is.' The sure and certain outcome of such misdirected thinking is a significantly diminished prayer life which will decisively set us on the fast-track to a completely destroyed prayer life.

Therefore, as we begin these thirty days of prayer it would be prudent to determine what prayer is 'not' and exorcise such illusions out of our prayer life altogether. To begin that process, I would encourage you to take a few moments and reflect on the following.

What Prayer is Not

- The Cosmic Vending Machine. This orientation views God as a resource that dispenses whatever we ask for. Faith is the currency that dispenses the product that we are asking for. If the product is not dispensed we assume that the machine is broken, or God is not listening, or we didn't get the right code words in the right order, or we inadvertently pressed the wrong button, or some other ignorant belief. In this model we have taken prayer as this mechanical action shaped by a one-way relationship of showing up when we need something, with no intent of showing up to give something.

- The Laundry List. Our needs, agendas, desires, wishes, hopes, dreams, etc. are put into list form. Our list can be clean and tidy, or it can be entirely scattered and chaotic. Either way, the fundamental format for prayer becomes embedded in a repeated and incessant recitation of this list as some sort of sterile mantra. We show up to place an order. Once the order is placed, we have this misguided expectation (that we've confused with faith) that the delivery is well on its way. We then take our pencil in hand and wait in excited anticipation for God to deliver on our requests so that we can begin checking these items off in order to prepare the next list.

- A Spiritual Panic Attack. This type of prayer is related to a current crisis. We have come to prayer in response to an emergency or some life event that is catastrophic at some level. We are in crisis. Our lives are in jeopardy or there has been a painful turn of events that has collapsed our world in some form and sent us reeling. The gravity of the crisis is beyond our personal resources and we are forced to seek out a resource more expansive than our own. Once the crisis has passed, we have this renewed sense that "we've got this." God is then relegated to a role akin to a first responder that we dial up when the next crisis hits.

- Manipulation. We come to prayer with the intent of having our desires fulfilled rather than exploring through prayer what our desires should be. We've already determined what's in our best interest and now we're trying to figure out how to get whatever we've determined that to be. So we have to be shrewd about all of this. We need to be convincing. We have to create a credible rationale to move God in our direction. We've got to sell God on these ideas of ours. These prayers are agenda driven, they're done with the intent to achieve our particular goals rather than joining God in His goals, and they humanize God by assuming that He's gullible.

- Bargaining. This type of prayer is where the individual attempts to strike a bargain with God. We make promises of some kind of improved behavior, or the abandonment of old behaviors, or assurances of a greater devotion to prayer, or a fuller commitment to family, or the giving up of an addiction, or the pledging of money or some other resource. The intent is to wrangle and deliver a sales pitch where God derives something out of the deal that makes it sufficiently compelling for Him to comply.

- Biblical Coercion. This type of prayer takes the authority and principles outlined in scripture and editorializes them sufficiently to suit the agenda of the individual. This is an effort to press God into service on our behalf based on the promises He has given us in scripture as we have chosen to interpret them. In essence, we are attempting to back God into a corner by using the edited version of His own words against Him in order to lend sufficient credence to our agenda.

- Unprayed Prayers. There are prayers that we have not prayed. There are those things that we have withheld from God because we don't believe that He will answer, or we have some sense that the answer is not likely to be favorable. We feel the weight of shame so we would rather keep everything hidden deep under the pain of our guilt. We sense that we have repeatedly failed God in some inexcusable way and therefore feel unworthy to bring anything before Him. Unprayed prayers are those things that we have unnecessarily withheld for any number of reasons. Such a choice can diminish the whole of our prayer life and rob us of what God is standing ready to do in our lives.

- Testing of God. Many times our prayers are a means of testing God. It's an experiment to either prove or disprove His existence. Is He real? If He is, does He love me enough to follow-through? Does He care enough to give me what I 'think' I need? Will He take the time to listen to 'little-old-me?' Am I important enough for God to turn aside from all of His obligations and sit with me? Is this real to the point that I can dare to stake my life on it? This is a manifestation of our attempt to build our faith in a manner where our faith becomes dependent upon the very thing that we were errantly using to build it.

There are many things that prayer is not. These are simply a handful that I have seen in my life and in the life of so many others. Oddly, we are often not fully aware of these. They have become so engrained as part of our personal theology, and so habitually integrated by virtue of our actions that we often do them unawares. As you move forward in this book, I would encourage you to be aware of these should they emerge in your prayer life.

Section One

Chapter 3

What Prayer Is

*"It is the person of prayer who shakes the world.
And it is when our knees hit the ground
in prayer that the shaking begins."*

– Craig D. Lounsbrough

A Handful of Notable Quotes - What Prayer Is

I have structured this chapter by including a series of quotes from those individuals who have immersed themselves in the rich discipline of prayer. These are the individuals who can speak to what prayer is far better than most. These persons of faith have grasped the essential essence of prayer and stated it in ways that break all lesser ideas of what prayer is and what we're doing when we engage in it.

This selection represents people from across the span of human history. They embody the human experience as lived out over thousands of years. They come from differing backgrounds. Their roles in carrying out the faith varied, but the manner in which they lived out their faith was the same. These are some of the giants of the faith who became giants because they made prayer an unalterable foundation in their lives.

At the end of this chapter I have included a handful of my own quotes so that you might understand my heart as you navigate this book in the days ahead. As such, I would encourage you to sit with these quotes and let them shape you as God sees fit. I would hope that they ignite a fresh and wholly energizing view of prayer that lifts the power of prayer off of the pages that follow and infuses that power into every part of your life.

"I pray because I can't help myself. I pray because I'm helpless. I pray because the need flows out of me all the time, waking and sleeping. It doesn't change God. It changes me."
~ C.S. Lewis

"We must remember that the shortest distance between our problems and their solutions is the distance between our knees and the floor."
~ Charles Stanley

"Whether we realize it or not, prayer is the encounter of God's thirst with ours. God thirsts that we may thirst for him."
~ St. Augustine

"Prayer does not fit us for the greater work; prayer is the greater work."
~ Oswald Chambers

"Prayer is simply talking to God—and the most important thing I can say about this is that God wants you to talk to Him!"
~ Billy Graham

"I have been driven many times upon my knees by the overwhelming conviction that I had nowhere else to go. My own wisdom and that of all about me seemed insufficient for that day."
~ Abraham Lincoln

"I have so much to do that I shall spend the first three hours in prayer."
~ Martin Luther

"Long as they live should Christians pray, for only while they pray they live."
~ Dwight L. Moody

"True prayer is neither a mere mental exercise nor a vocal performance. It is far deeper than that - it is spiritual transaction with the Creator of Heaven and Earth."
~ Charles Spurgeon

"Prayer is invading the impossible."
~ Jack Hayford

"Is prayer your steering wheel or your spare tire?"
~ Corrie ten Boom

A Collection of Craig's Quotes on Prayer

What Prayer Is

"Prayer penetrates the underside of heaven and sends the full force of an invisible realm hurdling against the adversaries that are too naïve to understand what's about to descend upon them."

"I am convinced beyond words to convey that prayer is infinitely more than the mindless ranting of some poor, delusional soul talking to some imaginary friend in some imaginary place. Oh, to the contrary. Prayer is the manifest pleading of a soul worn raw that, by the simple act of prayer, unleashes untold forces that we can't imagine that surge in a descent so massive and so inconceivably powerful that the ground of everything before them shakes. And in this descent lives are changed beyond recognition, nations are transformed beyond comprehension, and history is brought to its knees in the face of a God who says, "be healed." That, my friend, is nothing of a delusional soul or imaginary friend or any other such nonsense."

"How do I tell you what prayer is? It is everything that I need every time I kneel in the practice of it. It shakes the infinite alive and sets its armies afoot in defense of me. It will never run aground or find itself drowning in the waters of the adversity that I bring to it. Nothing it faces is insurmountable, for to think that such an adversary exists is to run a fool's errand. It will shield me in its advance, it will beckon me to anticipate the miracles that it is about to wield, and in the midst of it all it calms me as it whispers, "Be still and know that I am God." And because of these reasons and a million more, I find prayer the single greatest place that I could ever imagine being."

"Prayer is where I trade the rhetoric of men the for the promises of God. It is where I petition perfection instead of counting on those who somehow survived an election. It is to accept the incomprehensible invitation of God to have this weak voice of mine thunder down the halls of heaven and roll up to the throne of the God of all eternity so that as small as I am, I might have an audience with this "King of kings." It is where my fatigue becomes a stage upon which God can unveil His strength in stunning fashion, and where my fear is obliterated by His courage. Prayer is where I rise above this tangled world and find myself enveloped by a world that I visit today but will live in tomorrow. Prayer is utterly indispensable to this cringing existence, for unless I rise above it I will be consumed by the darkness of it. Prayer is this and does this and will always be this."

And finally…

"Too often we have stripped our single greatest asset of its power and hobbled it to the degree that it has come to be viewed only as a pathetic last resort. Yet despite our incessant meddling, this asset nonetheless remains a first resort so potent that it never needs a last one. And that asset is prayer."

As I have in previous chapters, I would suggest that as part of your reorientation regarding prayer that you sit with these words for a bit. Ponder them. Pray over them. Draw them into your spiritual disciplines, particularly that of prayer.

What is prayer to you?

____

____

____

____

____

____

____

Section One

Chapter 4

Obstacles to Prayer

"I want to live a life where prayer is the first thing that I do, the second thing, the third thing, and the last thing after the prayer has been answered."

~Craig D. Lounsbrough

Many of the obstacles to prayer are things that we have not given sufficient attention to or presume as somehow normal, appropriate, or of no real concern. They are the things that cleverly present themselves as rather casual issues that are of little importance. In our largely contrived busyness, we have hastily underestimated their importance and have assigned them to some place of irrelevance until we can get to them (which we rarely do). Therefore, seated all around us are destructive factors that lay hidden in the fields of our ignorance.

These things represent a less than disciplined understanding as to how God has called us to live out our lives. Yet, despite the fact that we have sidelined these destructive factors, they have sufficient potency and ample power to block our prayers. As such, we should not live unawares of such subtle power sitting hidden all around us. Rather, we should set out on a hunt for them, rigorously ferret them out, and then exorcise them out of our lives.

In this chapter we have outlined a handful of these destructive factors that too often lay hidden in our lives. And in wondering how or why our prayer lives seem so ineffectual, we might ask if any of these factors have found a place of residence in our lives.

Obstacles to Prayer

Sin. Sin is an intentional living outside of the will of God that places us at odds with who God created us to be. Sin is described as "anything that separates us from God." If we are engaging in such behaviors, we come to prayer separated from the God to Whom we are praying.

Self-Centered Agendas. We tend to live out our lives based on our agendas and our perception of what is in our best interest. Therefore, we do not come to prayer seeking God's direction, will, insights, and perspective. Rather, we come with a prepared agenda where we wrangle with God in order to achieve these agendas or obtain the resources to achieve them.

Distractions. Prayer becomes the thing that we squeeze into the many demands in our lives. It's something that sits somewhere near the bottom of the rather extensive checklist that outlines our obligations and duties. We intend to give prayer space and time, but it often falls prey to the many other demands that press prayer off of our calendar.

Our Perspective of Prayer. Often, we have developed an understanding of prayer as something that has value, but something that can be missed without extensive consequence to our lives. We don't see it as interacting with the God of the universe as an integral part of growing in relationship with Him and profoundly living out our lives in that relationship. It is more a prescribed duty that (if fulfilled) is optimal. But should time not permit, there is little lost in the absence of it.

Shiny Object and Squirrels. There are many things that vie for our attention, and we give many of those things that very attention. In reality, most of those things are not imperative to life and living, although we grant them that exact status. It is often assumed that if something in our life demands our attention it is because ignoring it will have dire consequences, when in fact deferring the majority of these things is unlikely to result in any consequence of consequence. Therefore, we rank these things as to their perceived importance as well as the pressing nature of whatever they might be demanding of us. As such, in the perpetual bombardment of a busy life, prayer is easily set aside.

Lack of Faith. We are lacking in faith. Prayer is understood within the context of the faith with which we use it. The lack of faith either inhibits our prayers as we feel that we bring very little to the process, or we bring little to the process because we don't necessarily believe in it. We forget that coming to prayer regardless of our level of faith is in itself the exhibition of faith. We must remember that the size of our faith only becomes an issue when we refuse to use the faith that we have.

Unmet Expectations. We come to prayer with expectations regarding the outcome of our prayers, or what we wish to obtain by praying. If those outcomes are not achieved (in light of the greater outcomes that God has for us), we feel that prayer is ineffectual or irrelevant. If it fails to generate our prescribed outcomes we are quick to label it as irrelevant or entirely powerless. Our assumptions rest in the belief that our expectations are the ones that are right for our situation, rather than being the one's that we should explore in order to determine what might actually be right for us.

A Jaded Heart. God has not answered our prayers in the way that we wanted, or in the time frame that we wanted, or maybe He didn't answer them at all (which is an answer, but not the one that we hoped for). We have found God disappointing, demanding, a less than generous God, and one that crushes our desires despite how passionately we bring them to Him. We refuse to understand that God cannot fulfill many of our desires because it is the fulfilling that would do the crushing. Therefore, we either refuse to pray any longer, or we do so in such a limited fashion that it can barely be defined as prayer.

The Lure of the World. The world is chock full of enticing things that have no depth and lack any substance whatsoever. And therein lies the absurdity of it all. In some breathless fashion we chase after that which we believe will do the things that we're chasing them to do. And once we actually catch them (or in some cases realize that we can't because nobody does), we're struck with the chafing reality that these things weren't what they appeared to be, or they didn't possess the resources that we had errantly endowed them with. But without missing a beat, we immediately set out to chase the next thing for the exact same reasons. And prayer goes wanting.

The Insurance Policy. Is prayer some supplemental thing that we do out of guilt, or a sense of obligation, or to cover the holes that we might have left in our efforts to tidy up our lives? Is prayer the means by which we ensure that our efforts are pushed through to our satisfaction in case we didn't push quite hard enough? Is prayer that safety net that we keep in place just in case the world fails us, or we fail ourselves? Is prayer that supplemental insurance policy that we hold onto 'just in case?' Prayer is not insurance. Rather, it's the assurance that we won't need insurance.

There are many things that create obstacles to our prayer. And maybe one of the biggest is our unwillingness to look for them. Either way, we would be wise to thoughtfully inventory our lives and ferret out anything that would create and sustain any such obstacle regardless of what it might be.

What are your obstacles?

____

____

____

____

____

____

____

____

Section One

Chapter 5

Additional Suggestions
My Own Personal Strategies – Structuring an Effective Prayer Life

"I think that one of the greatest prayers to pray is to ask for sufficient wisdom to pray the right prayers."

- Craig D. Lounsbrough

Prayer is intentional. So is our preparation for it. We would be wise to invest time and energy in structuring our lives in a manner that both sustains and perpetuates a bold and thoughtful prayer life.

Over the years, these are several of the things that I have found helpful in achieving those exact goals. I would suggest that you build them into your prayer life.

Have a Designated Place to Pray

Find that place in your house or apartment that becomes the place where you meet God. When you do this, this place takes on an aura or a sense that this is where you encounter God. This is where both of you meet up. The feeling that this is the place where you meet God can enhance your prayer time, add vitality to it, and make it easier to be consistent.

Have a Designated Time to Pray

While we are to pray throughout the day, find one time that is exclusively your time with God. Once you find it, protect it. While mornings tend to be busy for most people, try to find a time at the beginning of your day as you are more rested during that time. In addition, the act of prayer sets a balanced and energized tone for your day that nothing else can set in such a potent and sustaining manner.

Distractions

Unless your house is on fire or somebody's dying, things can wait. We have this pressing sense that we've got to get things done and check them off of our list. There's something critical about doing that. Otherwise, we'll be dwelling on everything that we need to do once we're done praying instead of focusing on the fact that we're praying. And in taking time with God we have set the stage for God to step in and take care of everything on our list in ways that are far more efficient and thorough than we could have imagined.

Track Scriptures in Your Bible as God Gives Them to You

Have a Bible where you can track scriptures that God brings to you, or ones that you discover throughout the day, or ones that a friend gives you. Underline them in your Bible, place the date by them, and mark the page with a sticky note. Begin to build a journal that outlines your prayer journey, thereby giving your prayer life a multi-dimensional sense that extends beyond this single moment of prayer.

Have Some Accompanying Material

Have something that you read daily or possibly weekly as part of your prayer time. This could be a pamphlet, a regular devotional, a newsletter, an article that you found of value, a chapter in a book, etc. Have these to refer to as part of your time with God to deepen and broaden the experience.

Your State of Mind

Realize that some days you might come to prayer very focused. Other days, you might be far more scattered. Some days you might have a strong sense of what you want to pray about, and at other times you may not. Simply bring who you are at that moment. It's not so much what you showed up with, it's the fact that you showed up.

To End Your Day

Have some Bible reading at the end of your day to round out your day. This could be a devotional, or part of reading through a particular book of the Bible, a "One Year Bible," or referencing a scripture that you read during your time in the morning. Bring a close to your day that helps to settle the demands that you experienced that day.

Conclusion

It is my prayer that 'prayer' becomes a central feature in your life. Life can difficult. It can come at us in ways entirely unexpected, and it can do so with absolutely no remorse. We can watch spouses walk away, standby as careers vanish in an instant, helplessly watch our children destroy their lives, wrestle with unrelenting addictions, fall deep into the throes of depression, be relentlessly haunted by trauma, witness the betrayal of friends, hate who we are, hate who we are becoming, and so much more. Life can be hard. Very hard. Extremely hard.

But prayer is the empowerment in the midst of our impoverishment. It is the hope when all other supposed 'hopes' fail us (as they will). It is the living lifeline to our God. It is the most under-used asset in our arsenal. It is power beyond our understanding and deliverance beyond our abilities. If we've been foolish enough to underestimate the power of prayer, then we've probably been naive enough to overestimate the power of everything else. Therefore, from this point forward may we take it upon ourselves to pray as we never have before, so that we might change our world as never before.

May God bless you in the thirty days ahead, and for every day that comes after that.

Notes:

____

____

____

____

____

____

____

____

____

Section 2

30 Days of

Prayer

Day 1

Betrayal Is the Manifestation of Someone's Greed, not a Commentary of Our Worth

"After saying these things, Jesus was troubled in his spirit, and testified, 'Truly, truly, I say to you, one of you will betray me."

~John 13:21

Betrayal is intentional…ruthlessly so. It is the deliberate choice of someone to hold their interests as so superior to our well-being that the cost of crushing us in order to advance their agendas is deemed as entirely reasonable and indisputably acceptable. In this horrifically devastating scenario, we become fodder in someone's blind pursuit of objectives that such an action will, in fact, never achieve.

Once the perpetrator comes to understand that both the agenda and the means chosen to achieve it accomplish neither, they will quickly fabricate a distorted narrative crafted to sustain the acceptability of what they've done. Such a short-sighted effort will demand repeated editing as the narratives cannot keep step with the ever-emerging realities of the betrayal. And herein the betrayal multiplies as the increasingly frustrated perpetrator fruitlessly attempts to justify choices that are ever more intensely being revealed as flawed, failed, and beyond the scope of every fresh iteration.

Yet, we are not human fodder. Betrayal is not a reflection of who 'we' are. It is, in fact, a reflection of who 'they' are. And although the person who betrayed us will adamantly deny such a reality, we must remember that this is simply a failed means by which the betrayer will work to justify unjustifiable actions. You are not human fodder. You are not refuse to be discarded at someone else's whim. Quite the opposite…you are a child of God. You are a manifestation of His amazing ingenuity. You are cherished royalty. You are a one-of-a-kind person with a one-of-a-kind calling. That is who you are.

"Each and every day take the time to tell your children the great people that they are so that they don't grow up living each and every day thinking they're the bad people that they're not."

~ Craig D. Lounsbrough

Morning Prayer

Dear God:
It is likely that the one who betrayed me is already experiencing the pain of an agenda not achieved and is even now working diligently to avoid that reality. I know that they will work to keep the consequences of their choices at bay, and I know that they will ultimately fail in achieving that goal. And whatever all of this does to them, it is my prayer that they may surrender to those realities and in doing so find their way to You.

As for me, heal the wounds within me, for they are deep. You say that You "heal the brokenhearted and bind up their wounds," and I believe that You're doing that right now because You promised to. And in the healing, may I come to understand myself better, may I grow as I press in and through this time in my life, and may I find myself turning to You with an ever-increasing intensity and ever-growing commitment. I know that my heart will be peppered with hate and I will tend toward revenge as that is part of my humanity. But as this happens, build within me an ability to see the other person as a wounded human being who has only served to increase their own woundedness. And may that soften me sufficiently to begin to forgive them, knowing that such an action will not come easily, but it will come.

I pray all of this in Jesus's Name. Amen.

A Thought to Carry with Me Today

"No betrayal is so big that God's commitment to us and presence within us is not bigger."

~ Craig D. Lounsbrough

Before this day, I release to God...

____

____

____

____

____

____

____

____

____

____

Evening Prayer

Dear God:
As this day closes, so does my anger and my hatred. I believe that throughout this day You have been at work in my heart. I thank You for a steady healing, as incremental as it may be at times. I thank You that You are building within me the ability to forgive even though I am very resistant to it at times. And I am deeply appreciative that You are gradually creating within me the ability to see the amazing future that You have already created for me.

With You, an ending is always a beginning and it is never otherwise. And as I end this day, I look forward to the beginning of tomorrow and every tomorrow after that. Grant me a peaceful sleep that arises from a peaceful mind and ever-settling heart.

I pray all of this in Jesus' Name. Amen.

A Thought to Prepare for Tomorrow

"I cannot begin to tell you how many times I have come to prayer broken far beyond any conceivable hope of repair. I have likewise come without anywhere to turn simply because, much like myself, everything around me lies broken beyond repair. And I cannot tell you how many times God has taken that which is broken and has used it to do what could never have done should any of that had been whole."

~ Craig D. Lounsbrough

From this day, I release to God...

Day 2

The Aching Void of an Absent Parent

"Even if my father and mother abandon me, the LORD will hold me close."

~ Psalm 27:10

There are many things that are meant to be forever. There are those things whose permanence in our lives is never questioned because they are designed to be permanent. Their role in our lives had nothing of a temporary nature built into them. Therefore, we have no reason to doubt their permanence. As such, we never stop to consider what life would be like without them because such a thought is entirely at odds with their permanence. Yet, we live in a world where permanence can be traded for lesser agendas and what should never have left us does.

When a parent abandons us, the immense internal conflict of their supposed permanence as held in juxtaposition against their absence rocks our world to dark places. In our desperate efforts to correlate the irreconcilable discrepancies of permanence as held against abandonment, we rationalize the loss of the parent or we work to suppress the pain by denying the loss altogether. We work to believe that this might be better anyway, or that they were going to leave sooner or later, or that they needed their space to live their lives. Yet we soon discover that no rationalization is ever big enough or convincing enough to release someone of a commitment for which there is no release.

And in the desperation of times like these we begin to realize that we've turned to God because He has remained permanent. It is His permanence that becomes our sure refuge. Our sense of stability arises from His stability. Our ability to somehow craft a future empty of a parent that should have been part of that crafting is centered on the fact that God is a certain part of that future as much as He is a part of the present that is shaping that future. And we have the certainty that He will never abandon us in either.

"At the point that I can look into my children's faces and say that my life is about their lives, I have finally come to the point that I can now start becoming a parent. And if I've not reached this point, I might be a parent by birth but it all ends there."

~ Craig D. Lounsbrough

Morning Prayer

Dear God:
I am lonely. The people that were supposed to be here…are not. You know the reasons that they've left, and You know the hole within me that their departure has created. You know how dark this hole is and how impossible it feels that it will ever be filled. You also know the hole within them that caused them to leave. You know that the hole within them will never be filled by their choices. And You know that even though the hole within them and the hole within me are very different, they are both in desperate need of healing.

And so, I'm asking You to fill the hole within both of us. You know that it's hard for me to pray for the hole within them, but I know that for myself to heal in the way that I want to heal I must pray for their healing as well. They ran 'to' something because they were running 'from' something. Help them stop the running and start the healing.

Dear God, I believe that You can do more than just fill the hole. You said that you will "supply all [my] need according to [Your] riches in glory by Christ Jesus." This need is big. It's bigger than any collection of words could ever hope to explain. But You are bigger. So, I'm counting on You to fill this hole, heal it, and use this experience to grow me, deepen me, better root me in You, and position me to reach others for You in ways that I could not have done so were it not for this hole.

I pray all of this in Jesus' Name. Amen.

Before this day, I release to God...

____

____

____

____

____

____

____

____

A Thought to Carry with Me Today

"Dear God, I commit to remember
that the absence of a parent never
means the absence of You."
~ Craig D. Lounsbrough

Evening Prayer

Dear God:
Tonight, the hole is still there. But I know that You have worked out Your healing throughout the day, and You have filled it bit by bit. The journey to healing is a long one, and while that bothers me, I accept it. As much as I don't like that reality, I know that it is within the journey to healing that we grow. And although I am frequently resistant, I am willing to take that journey because You have promised to take it with me every step of the way. And I have the confidence of knowing that You will never step away.

Thank You for being my Heavenly Father. You are the Infinite Parent. The Forever Father. And I know that the day will come when I will be able to approach Your great throne, crawl into the warm expanse of Your lap, and feel the embrace of a Heavenly Father who is Himself filled with the joy of filling me. On that day, all holes will end…forever. And I am thankful for that.

I pray all of this in the Name of Jesus. Amen.

A Thought to Prepare for Tomorrow

"I might have my holes, but the healing of today means that they will be smaller in every tomorrow, including the one that is now only hours away."

~ Craig D. Lounsbrough

From this day, I release to God...

Day 3

Being Jesus to a Gender Confused Culture

"I praise you because I am fearfully and
wonderfully made; your works are wonderful,
I know that full well."
~ Psalm 139:14

One of the worst things is not knowing who you are. And probably a close second to that is to hate what you do know. And right behind that there's the effort to create something that you think you'll like in order to solve both of those problems.

But all of this misses the only battle that's worth fighting, and the only effort that will insure success. Life is not about creating ourselves. Rather, it's about discovering ourselves. It's not about assuming some presumed right to make ourselves what we're not. Rather, it's about the privilege of discovering who we already are. And that journey is one of the most profound journeys that we are each privileged to take.

Yet we live in a world bent on creating what cannot be created. Certainly, we can mimic many things, but the mimicking will never make us those things. We stand by and watch those committed to becoming what they are not, realizing that the greatest pain experienced by these persons is not the struggle of loving themselves. Rather, it's the heartbreaking failure that they will experience in the persistent effort to make themselves what they are not. And the self-hatred that is certain to follow that failure will handily surpass that which drove them to this decision in the first place.

The rampant declaration to pursue such agendas and to force them on larger society illustrates the failed nature of the endeavor. It would be wise to remember that if something is based in truth it will not need us to sell it simply because the priceless nature of truth always places it beyond the reach of any such market. And one of the greatest truths that we are in desperate need of embracing is the truth of who we are, along with the equally great truth of who we are not.

"You can borrow an identity if you want. But that's something akin to spending the whole of your life in a fitting room full of clothes that never fit because you're embarrassed by the ones that do".

~ Craig D. Lounsbrough

Morning Prayer

Dear God:
There are those who can't find who they are, or who have found themselves and are running from what they've found. These people are spending their lives trying to become something that they are not because they don't like what they see. I know that our greatest satisfaction and most profound life is found is discovering who You created us to be and then spending our lives cultivating that person. I know that these are hurting people. Confused people. People embracing a path of failure. People who do not believe that who they are is adequate, appealing, authentic, or worth discovering.

I ask that You help these people come face-to-face with their true, authentic selves. And in that encounter, I ask that You help them engender a robust excitement for who they are and who that true self has the potential of becoming. Help them see the beautiful, entirely unique, and utterly fascinating person that they already are. Help them to understand that they are "fearfully and wonderfully made" in a way that they cannot afford to abandon, forsake, or diminish through lesser choices.

God, I pray for these people, as well as the ones who are watching them walk a road to their own demise. Lord, cause them to fall desperately and deeply in love with who You made them to be.

I pray all of this in Jesus' Name. Amen.

A Thought to Carry with Me Today

"Today I will look for Your fingerprint in everything around me instead of creating footprints that all lead away from me."

~ Craig D. Lounsbrough

Before this day, I release to God…

____

____

____

____

____

____

Evening Prayer

Dear God:
Today they were people who spent their resources working to create themselves rather than discover themselves. I know that they may have felt some temporal satisfaction and accomplishment in these efforts. But I also know that these feelings only belie the deeper reality that to create oneself is only to cheat oneself. They will likely not hear that from me. But I believe that they can hear that from You.

So tonight, touch their lives. Grant them an increased sense of self-appreciation rather than self-condemnation. Allow them Lord, to begin to discover who You created them to be, to find themselves enthralled and utterly captivated with that person, to be helplessly caught up in the possibilities that lay both in them and in front of them, and then grant them the resources to grow that person into Your image.

I pray all of this in the Name of Jesus. Amen.

A Thought to Prepare for Tomorrow

"Although what I see in the mirror often doesn't fit who I believe myself to be, that person provides me everything that I need to be everything that I am. And I have been granted the privilege of spending every minute of my tomorrow with that person."

~ Craig D. Lounsbrough

From this day, I release to God…

Day 4

Wrestling With the Discouragement of Failure

"…for all have sinned and fallen short
of the glory of God."
~ Romans 3:23

Failure. It's having set out to do something, or not do something, and having failed to achieve the goal either way. It's falling short. It's having missed the mark, or having pulled out of the race long before we came anywhere close to the mark. It's the dream that we couldn't breathe life into, or the fear that we couldn't breathe the life out of. It's the relationship that we couldn't hold because we were not worth being held. It's the thing that puts us in our place because we foolishly thought that we might be better than that place. It's falling down and finding no reason to get back up.

Failure is a stark message regarding our ability or lack thereof. It is the undeniable evidence of what we feared might be true, that we are in fact inadequate or incompetent or whatever we feared that we might be. It reminds us of our misdirected efforts to elevate our place in life, and it assigns us the very station that we worked so hard to avoid. It tells us that our dreams are bigger than our ability to achieve them. That mediocrity is our lot in life, so we'd be wise to settle there and at least do that well.

But we forget that failure is the refusal to try. Trying and not succeeding is the very place where God has placed the richest cache of learning opportunities available to us. It's a chance to try again, but to try differently. It's an opportunity to become everything that failure says we cannot become because it is failure itself that has taught us how to outflank it. Falling short, missing the mark, or pulling out of the race are nothing more than events packed rich with learning opportunities that set the stage for greater things…possibly great things. It is not the fact that these things happened. It is what we do with the fact that they happened. And if we seize the opportunities for growth that God has graciously planted within each of these, failure will fall to a life rich with success.

"Failure is the prerequisite to success,
not the elimination of it."
~ Craig D. Lounsbrough

Morning Prayer

Dear God:
I know that failure is the lie told by men without vision. For I know that You have placed growth opportunities in everything. And I pray that I can be wise enough to seek them out until I find them, learn from them until I know their lessons well, and then apply them until I have forcefully drawn every morsel of growth out of them.

My failures are many. Many. And maybe the most painful ones are those that I walked away from without harvesting the bountiful lessons that You had embedded within them. I confess that I have failed here. But where I have probably failed the most is believing that You will never fail me. Despite the fact that I've given far less than I should, that I've compromised my values in order to bypass the work involved in defending them, that I've chosen the easy road which never runs to You, and that I've betrayed others including You in order to advance myself…if I have failed You, it is here.

But it is not my failures that are Your focus. It is my redemption. It is my pursuit of You that is enlivened by Your pursuit of me. It is Your relentless commitment to salvaging what I've made of my life, and then constructing something wildly phenomenal out the wreckage. Despite it all, You've never failed me. Not once. Not ever. May I become what You are. May I become faithful, trustworthy, ever reliable, and always obedient. "Help me overcome my unbelief," so that I might be empowered to do these things so that I will never fail at doing great things.

In pray all of this in Jesus' Name. Amen.

A Thought to Carry With Me Today

"Failure is opportunity. As such, I am never surrounded by a bunch of failures. Rather, I am engulfed by a mass of opportunity."

~ Craig D. Lounsbrough

Before this day, I release to God…

____

____

____

____

____

Evening Prayer

Dear God:
Today some things didn't work out. I fell short…probably shorter than I should have. I confess these to You tonight. But beginning tonight…beginning right now I am asking You to show me the precious lessons buried in these less than success efforts. And may You grant me the wisdom to apply these lessons in a way that uses each of them to the fullest.

Forgive me for being less than I should have been and help me to be more than I can be. May tomorrow morning be the dawning of a day where the growth that You wish to achieve in my life will exceed anything that would serve to stand against that growth. And I pray that into the lives of those around me as well. I pray that into the crippled souls of people for whom failure seems to be the whole of their identity and the entirety of their story. Free them from their sense of failure as I am asking You to free me.

I pray all of this in the Name of Jesus. Amen.

A Thought to Prepare for Tomorrow

"Tomorrow I will have an entire day to squeeze incredible lessons out of my worst failures. And therefore, my plan is to start squeezing early."

~ *Craig D. Lounsbrough*

From this day, I release to God...

Day 5

The Agonizing Tragedy of Suicide

"Do you not know that your body is a temple of the Holy Spirit, who is in you, whom you have received from God? You are not your own; you were bought at a price. Therefore honor God with your body."

~ I Corinthians 6:19-20

Life is precious. Therefore, the loss of it goes deep. There are losses that are a natural part of our existence. They hurt, but at least they make sense. But then there are the losses that don't make sense. The losses that didn't need to happen. The losses that were premature, unnecessary, avoidable, and entirely out of step with life as we know it (or would like to know it).

Suicide is one of these. This loss was a choice. In all likelihood it involved the convergence of many things dark and weighty; hopelessness, despair, life gone wrong, self-hatred, incessant failures, the inability to find a niche, dreams smashed, relationships lost, faith gone. And the pressing compilation of such things tips the scales and renders death preferable to life. At some point of darkest desperation, a decision is made and an action is taken. And suddenly we are left with a loss that doesn't make sense. A loss that didn't need to happen. A loss that was premature and unnecessary. A loss that doesn't fit because it shouldn't. And despite our best effort to understand it all, resolution eludes us and people continue to die.

And all of those who live out their lives in those places are eventually left asking the question of "why?" But maybe we need to replace the question of "why" with the question of "how" because that question holds the answers to what we need to change in our lives, our families, our communities, and our nation to save the next life.

"Although the limb fell to the weight of winter's snow, the tree did not. And as I deal with my losses, I work to remember that I may lose a limb, but a limb is never a tree."

~ Craig D. Lounsbrough

Morning Prayer

Dear God:
Yes, I want to heal from those I've lost through suicide. But I don't want to heal so much that I forget the desperation that can cause a human being to forsake the privilege of living. I want to be sensitive to how difficult life can be and how fragile all of us can become, including myself.

Help me to hate it when the gift of life is snatched away at the hands of the very one to whom this gift was given. But more than that, help me to love the person so much, and to see the value in the life that they lived that they never become identified by the choice that they made. Rather, might they always be identified by the person that they were.

Today, right now, there are many, many people who are weighing out the value of their lives as held against the suffering in their lives. And in the weighing, they are finding little reason to live. Remind them that they are made in Your image, and that such an image is something at which to marvel.

And so, I ask You to crush the dark voices within these people. In their place, I ask You to speak into their lives an equally formidable sense of their worth, their value, and their immense potential. I am asking You to create a compelling feeling of self-love within them, a surging passion for life that won't be denied, an electrifying vision for their existence, and a belief that they have a place that no one can fill but them.

I pray all of this in Jesus' Name. Amen.

A Thought to Carry with Me Today

"I was created for the simple reason that
to not be created was unthinkable."
~ Craig D. Lounsbrough

Before this day, I release to God...

Evening Prayer

Dear God:
Despite my prayers, there are people who took their lives today. And there are families, friends, and communities that sit numbed and stunned tonight. There are those who will not sleep tonight, or for many nights to come. Those who are gone will never walk through the door with tales of their day. A chair will wait for someone who no longer needs a chair. A family will have to figure out how to be family with one voice silenced. A friend won't be showing up. The call will never come. The career will never happen. A future has now become a past.

Thank You for the life of this person. Thank You for the memories that will never die even though the person who made them has. Thank You that a precious bit of them remains in all of us. May we always hold the memory of that person over the choice of that person. And from this point forward may we find our own lives compelled to bring to our world what that person now cannot. May we make our worlds better so that their loss is offset by what You, dear God, can do with even the most shattering losses.

I pray all of this in the Name of Jesus. Amen.

A Thought to Prepare for Tomorrow

"Make my life one that ignites a passion
to live in the lives of those who are
considering the choice not to live."

~ *Craig D. Lounsbrough*

From this day, I release to God...

Day 6

Discovering My Purpose

"Many are the plans in a person's heart, but it is the LORD's purpose that prevails."
~ Proverbs 19:21

Purpose. Without it, life has no meaning. Without it, life is empty. We can liberally pour all kinds of questionable things into our lives every day of our lives, but without purpose the emptiness remains despite the pouring. In fact, pour in the wrong stuff and the emptiness becomes more empty.

We are all created with an innate need for purpose that will not relent. A sense that we matter. A belief that in the chaos of life we have a purpose in the chaos. A conviction that we are here because to 'not' be here is an unacceptable option. A deep sense that we were created because not to be created was too great a mistake.

Many can argue that life is random and happenstance. Yet, that argument itself is neither random nor happenstance, which turns that argument back on itself. The reality is that the core needs of our shared humanity don't resonate with such a perspective. Such an argument makes our existence accidental. And such randomness strips us of any value, or purpose, or calling, or whatever it is that we might choose to call it.

We need a purpose. Not just something that we do, but something that we were created to do. Not a reason that we create for our existence, but the reason for which we were created. We need something that identifies who we are, the place that we are to occupy during this time in history into which we've been both called and inserted, and the impact that we're supposed to have while doing all of that.

Purpose is the great "why" as to our existence. It's the pristine goal, our truest north, our destination in a world that is always changing its destination based on preference, current trends, and flawed ideologies. You have a purpose that is uniquely yours. Yours for the taking. Yours for the living.

"If you've yet to find your purpose, maybe it's not that you don't have one. Rather, maybe it's that you haven't given it permission to find you. And you might ask, is there any legitimate purpose in that?"

~ Craig D. Lounsbrough

Morning Prayer

Dear God:
I wander…way too much. I live thinking that just living is the purpose of it all. What I've missed is that living is the thing that I do while I'm pursuing my purpose. My purpose makes living purposeful. Dear God, I don't know that I know what my purpose is, at least with any kind of specificity. However, You do.

I know that You created me "for such a time as this." And I know that I came into all of this as a marvelously complete package. Dear God, You are wildly ingenious. And I know You were brilliant enough to place within me everything that I need to be in order to do everything that You created me to do. I am complete, and I claim that right now.

I confess to You that I don't see all of that, and most times I don't believe it either. But You know that I want to believe it. Yet more than that, I want to act on it. I don't want to miss anything that You've created me to be, or anything that You created me to do. I want to be the sum total of everything that I am, and everything that I am purposed to do. So, help me find my purpose, help me to fall in love with it, and then help me to pursue it for the rest of my life.

I pray all of this in Jesus' Name. Amen.

A Thought to Carry with Me Today

"Right now I am making the choice to live out this day choosing to be intentional about not being unintentional."

~ Craig D. Lounsbrough

Before this day, I release to God...

____

____

____

____

____

____

____

____

____

Evening Prayer

Dear God:
I am going to bed knowing that I tried to be intentional about the way that I lived my life this day. At times the demands of the day got the better of me and I found myself scrambling to keep up. That's the craziness of my life sometimes. But dear God, I know that You have the ability to bring purpose out of whatever chaos I create. So, when my life gets chaotic and I'm too tired to keep a grip on the leash, even then Lord bring Your purpose out of that.

When I'm disobedient, or careless, or I let my darker desires get the better of me, even then Lord bring Your purpose out of my sin. Do not let me get in the way of my purpose. And so, tonight prepare me for a tomorrow where I will live in my purpose and less in my weakness.

I pray all of this in the Name of Jesus. Amen.

A Thought to Prepare for Tomorrow

"My purpose is waiting for me to step into it. And I should do that the moment that I step out of bed."

~ *Craig D. Lounsbrough*

From this day, I release to God...

Day 7

The Plague of Addictions

"Like a city whose walls are broken through is a person who lacks self-control."
~ Proverbs 25:28

Life is filled with pain. Or maybe more accurately, our lives are engulfed in pain. We've all run into it, or have had it run into us, or have had it run over us. That pain can be physical, emotional, mental, or spiritual. It can be a product of the people around us, or the person within us. It can come to us in the form of circumstances beyond our control, or circumstances that we should have controlled. We might have had nothing to do with it, or everything to do with it. In whatever way it comes, pain comes to all of us.

The perpetually debilitating nature of our pain gradually weakens our resolve to fight it. Our belief that we can somehow beat it dissolves into some sort of mythical fantasy that becomes dimmer with each passing day. Desperate to have even a moment of relief from the pain that dogs our steps, we turn to self-medication. Self-medication can take on any number of forms, but the desire to seek relief is what drives them all. If these methods of self-medication deliver the desired relief, our decision to use them is reinforced. In time, we can begin to develop a gradually increasing dependency upon them that is far beyond their intended use or actual benefit.

These means of self-medication soothe our emotional state, grant us a sense of control over our pain, and become so thoroughly integrated into our daily lifestyle that to remove them would cause a disruption in our lives that we perceive as far greater than the disruption of the dependency that we have now created. We soon discover that the means of self-medication has created its own pain. And in time that pain replaces the pain that we were originally self-medicating against, leaving us in the perpetually debilitating state that is certain to be our fate if we decide to swap one kind of pain for another in order to somehow remedy our pain.

The longer the dependency, the tighter its grip. We fear the seemingly insurmountable challenge of breaking the addiction. This fear is compounded by our concern that what we medicated ourselves against will return in force if we forsake our addiction. In essence, we are held hostage to a something that numbs but never cures.

"To free yourself from one cell to immediately rush to the next cell isn't getting you out of any prison."

~ Craig D. Lounsbrough

Morning Prayer

Dear God:
There are things that enslave me. I am bound by shackles of all kinds. I know what many of them are and I am tired of every one of them. But I also know that there are many that I'm not aware of. There are things that I've been bound by for so long that I've allowed them to become part of who I am and what I do. I am tired of the shackles.

And so Lord, whatever it is that binds me, whatever dependency I have that I've cultivated or given permission to, whatever the addiction is that I readily admit to or constantly deny…whatever these things are, I am asking You to free me from them. Free me from them in ways that I thought to be impossible. You said, "If the Son sets you free, you will be free indeed." Free me because I do not have the power nor the courage to be any kind of liberator by myself, for I fear that liberation from my addiction may open the door for me to be enslaved by that which I've spent my life running from.

The only thing that I want to serve in life is You. I want to give the entirety of myself to You and You alone, for in being surrendered to You I am freed from everything and to everything. Therefore, please take away all of the lesser things that I've allowed to enslave me and fill me with everything that will free me.

I pray all of this in Jesus' Name. Amen.

A Thought to Carry with Me Today

"Maybe it's not about breaking your shackles at all.
Maybe it's about making you bigger than anything
that would ever try to shackle you ever again."

~ Craig D. Lounsbrough

Before this day, I release to God...

____

____

____

____

____

____

____

Evening Prayer

Dear God:
Today the world came at me. And in its ever-typical way, it tried to place its shackles on me. It came after my heart, my mind, my relationships, my dreams, my career, my self-esteem…in essence, it came after me. But I refused it. Not perfectly. Not to the degree that maybe I wish I had. But I stood my ground to the best of my ability.

I am not enough to break the shackles that bind me, nor constantly fend off the ones that the world wishes to slap on my wrists. But that's why I'm praying to You tonight dear God. Because You break shackles, and You desire to make me bigger than any shackle this world can fashion. And so, I ask You to do both.

I pray all of this in Jesus' Name. Amen.

A Thought to Prepare for Tomorrow

"What will I do when all of my shackles lay shattered and broken at my feet? I will reach over and begin breaking the shackles of the person standing next to me. And I would challenge you to envision a world where we're all doing that every day."

~ *Craig D. Lounsbrough*

From this day, I release to God...

Day 8

The Painful Struggle of Infertility

"I will repay you for the years the locusts have eaten— the great locust and the young locust, the other locusts and the locust swarm— my great army that I sent among you."

~ Joel 2:25

What many people are desperate to have are the very things that others recklessly throw away. What is cherished, intimately longed for, and desperately sought after by so many is discarded by others without so much as a fleeting thought.

Such is the agonizing dilemma of those facing the pain of infertility. Having squarely set decades of dreams on the immense privilege of having a child, couples find their dreams brought to a jarring and often unexpected halt. Facing the brutal possibility of being childless, these couples expend massive amounts of time, emotional energy, and personal resources to salvage a dream that seems to slip further away with every attempt to save it.

Wildly gyrating emotions spin off sporadic thoughts of physical or personal inadequacy. We wonder if this is punishment for some perceived offense that is only now being executed on our passion to hold a child. Thoughts of injustice as held against the reality that life is unjust. An uninvited jealousy of other couples who were able to bear children that runs head-long against the very real joy that we have for them. And then, the brutal thought of those who recklessly abort the very thing that we would give the entirety our lives to hold. The turmoil is unspeakable. The pain unfathomable.

Life robs us in many ways. But God enriches us in every way. What the world takes, God will restore. We will never lose anything that God cannot and will not give back to us many times over. The shape and form of what He gives may not resemble what we lost, but it will provide the healing that we need. The truth of these statements will never and can never be offset by the depth, intensity, size, or pain of any loss…ever.

Morning Prayer

Dear God:
I know that life is full of loss. It's all around me and it's everywhere within me. In this world, we can't get away from it. I know that because I've done my level best to do exactly that. And despite those efforts, it seems like some sort of loss is always lying in wait just around the corner of every dream that I've ever had.

But Lord, sometimes the losses are so big, so deep, so life-altering, so unjust, so seemingly impossible to live with…so everything that they should not be that I have a hard time accepting them. The inability to conceive a child is one of those. I'm way too human and way too fragile to take the really brutal losses and somehow find a safe or reasonable place for them despite how much I want to do that.

You know life can be brutal. You're no stranger to any of that. You lived it. You endured it. You knew it was coming for You from the beginning of creation. You stepped into this world knowing that it was staring You in the face.

But knowing that kind of brutality, You said, "Blessed are those who mourn, for they shall be comforted." Dear God, fill the hole left by the hope of a child. I don't want to play the victim; I want to be the victor. I don't want to spend the rest of my life pouting; I want to live my days prevailing. I want to rest on the fact that nothing can be taken from me that You cannot replace many times over in whatever way You decide to do that. I desperately want to live with that reality, with that hope, and with that peace.

I pray all of this in Jesus's Name. Amen.

A Thought to Carry with Me Today

"If I have never had, or worse yet, I have lost the conviction that life (despite all of the blows it wields and the savagery that it spawns) is nonetheless an incalculable privilege, I will have in that single loss forfeited the whole of my life and effectively wiped out any hope that I can or will do anything other than exist."

~ *Craig D. Lounsbrough*

Before this day, I release to God...

____

____

____

____

____

____

Evening Prayer

Dear God:
Tonight I go to bed with empty arms that I had hoped would hold a child. This is one of many losses. Some of those losses are new, and some I've carried for a long, long time. And around the world, people are going to bed or waking up with losses themselves. The biggest loss that the world can ever experience is to miss who You are and what You did for us. That loss handily eclipses any loss, or possible combination of losses that we could ever experience.

So tonight, wherever they might be, I pray You into the losses that lay heavy on the lives of billions of people around the globe. Whatever losses they are going to bed with, or waking up to, I would ask You to be there in their midst to show them who You are so that they might never experience the greatest loss known to men…and that is to lose You. And may it be the same for me.

I pray all of this in Jesus' Name. Amen.

A Thought to Prepare for Tomorrow

"The losses in my life are so immense that I can barely stand and hardly breath. But I must remember that it is God who holds my hand and grants me breath. And because He does, the losses will eventually collapse for lack of breath."

~ Craig D. Lounsbrough

From this day, I release to God...

Day 9

The Plague of Low Self-Esteem

"For you created my inmost being; you
Knit me together in my mother's womb. I praise
you because I am fearfully and wonderfully made;
your works are wonderful, I know that full well."
~ Psalm 139:13-14

We have difficulty believing that we are "fearfully and wonderfully made." That's a hard one sometimes. We look into the mirror or our decisions, and all that we see are the numerous cracks and spidery fissures in that mirror that speak to the destruction wrought by those decisions. We glance into the mirror of our achievements, and what stares back at us are a host of failures so numerous that the mirror is packed tight with them. We peer into the mirror of our relationships only to have no one peering back at us. And if we wipe the mirror clean of all of that stuff and simply glance at our own reflection, we wish that mirrors were never invented.

We don't like ourselves a whole lot. But what we don't like often goes much deeper than that which any mirror can reflect back to us. What we don't like is how people have defined us, or how we let them do that. We don't like how they have projected their own issues on us. How they blamed us for their mistakes so that they didn't have to face them. We are left sullen and sad by expectations that we didn't even come close to meeting because they were designed not to be met. And in the end, this very convincing definition of ourselves is compiled from a bunch of stuff that is far more a compilation of everyone else who had something to do with us than it was about us.

It's hard to believe that we are more than what we perceive ourselves to be. It's difficult to embrace the reality that we are truly made in God's image. That stuff doesn't resonate. We don't see that in the mirror, even if we squint and lean into it. But the greatest truths about us often don't resonate because we have difficulty believing that we could actually be something so wonderful.

"If you're not all that fond of the image in
the mirror, don't get rid of the mirror. Rather,
get rid of the people that shaped what
you're seeing in the mirror."

~ Craig D. Lounsbrough

Morning Prayer

Dear God:
Please help me to like me. Or better yet…help me to love me. I'm not all that certain about how to do that. There's a lot of self-help stuff out there and catchy ideas to help build my self-esteem. It's all man-made stuff that never really addresses the heart stuff.

You made me, "fearfully and wonderfully." You uniquely designed me. You intentionally placed me here, at this exact time in history. There was something very intentional in the way that You did all of that. You have a purpose and a plan for me that is bigger than anything that I could imagine. And that purpose and that plan is uniquely gifted to me and me alone. That's the truth about me.

I confess to You that I don't feel that way…at all. I just can't wrap my head around that no matter how hard I try. All of that's beyond me. But I want to believe it. I want to know that there's something of great value sitting within me just waiting to be released. I want to see 'me' how You see me, not how others have caused me to see me. Show me who I am through Your eyes. Help me to see my reflection in Your mirror.

I pray all of this in Jesus's Name. Amen.

A Thought to Carry with Me Today

"Look in the mirror. Go ahead and look yet again. And look not at the reflection, for while this body of yours is marvelously complex in ways that continue to elude the reach of modern science, it is but a simple shell that holds the image of God within you. And if the shell is that grand, how much more what God has placed inside of it."

~ Craig D. Lounsbrough

Before this day, I release to God...

____

____

____

____

____

____

____

Evening Prayer

Dear God:
I want to wake up tomorrow and feel better about who I see in the mirror. In fact, I want to see me in Your mirror. Not mine. Not the mirror held up to me by people who used me to avoid their own issues. Not the mirror of friends who betrayed me, or a spouse who left me, or parents who rejected me. Not the mirror of failed opportunities, or poor decisions. Not the mirror of an insensitive boss, or coworkers who sacrificed me to advance their own careers.

From this day forward, hold Your mirror up in front of me. And if perchance someone tries to hold up some other mirror other than Yours, I ask You to smash it to pieces.

I pray all of this in Jesus' Name. Amen.

A Thought to Prepare for Tomorrow

"God has enough confidence in me to send
me on the mission that He has for me tomorrow.
Therefore, do I have confidence in His confidence?"

~ Craig D. Lounsbrough

From this day, I release to God...

Day 10

The Loss of Hope

"Therefore we do not lose heart. Though outwardly we are wasting away, yet inwardly we are being renewed day by day. For our light and momentary troubles are achieving for us an eternal glory that far outweighs them all. So we fix our eyes not on what is seen, but on what is unseen, since what is seen is temporary, but what is unseen is eternal."
~ 2 Corinthians 4:16-18

Hope. Life drains us of it. It almost seems that life is constantly on the hunt for what little bit of hope we might have left. And life knows exactly what to do in order to home in on it and destroy it. That might be a child gone rogue. An unfaithful spouse. A boss who's passed you up for a promotion three different times. Unexpected debt. A medical issue that only gets worse the more it gets treated. Promises broken. A turn of events that puts a cherished dream forever out of reach…and so on. Life targets that stuff to target our hope.

The issue is not that we lose hope. Most often, the issue is based on what we have chosen to hope in. We hope in many things that we have no business hoping in. We lean on teetering promises that appeal to some selfish streak in us. We haphazardly hitch our wagon to something that doesn't have any horses pulling it. We fall for brilliantly crafted sales pitches that promise something that they don't even possess. We get swept up in the meaningless verbiage of smooth talking people because sixty seconds of fantasy is better than an hour of reality. We're desperate for some shred of hope, and so we make choices without a shred of common sense.

It's not that hope doesn't exist. It's that it doesn't exist in the places that we end up looking for it. It's really quite easy. Our only real hope is in God. Everything else is a flimsy facsimile that will continue to pretend it's real long after it's failed us.

"I can tell you that God has repeatedly 'raised me up' in the middle of the innumerable situations where 'up' had become a hope lost in the darkness of the places to which I had fallen. And while that is the miracle of my story, it sits waiting to be the reality of yours."

~ Craig D. Lounsbrough

Morning Prayer

Dear God:
I don't know if I can hope again. Ever. There's just been too much heartbreak and too much disappointment. The human heart can only take just so much. There's that final time when we take what little bit of hope that we have left, we cautiously gather it up, and we invest that hope in something that ends up failing. I've had too many of those. And so, I don't know if I can sustain one more disappointment.

I know that You are God. And I know that Your promises are trustworthy. I know that there's no risk in You. But the trauma of hope broken, and dreams smashed, and relationships destroyed, and betrayal at every turn, and dreams upended, and the bleakness that has now become the essence of my existence…all of that sitting in me makes it hard to trust You.

And so, help me to hope in You. Help me to take one final shot at hope. Do not let me walk away from You because if I do, there truly is no hope.

I pray all of this in Jesus's Name. Amen.

A Thought to Carry with Me Today

"The darkness might keep us from seeing the hope around us, but it does not have the power to remove the hope around us."

~ *Craig D. Lounsbrough*

Before this day, I release to God...

Evening Prayer

Dear God:
I tried to hope in You today. I did. It was small because I couldn't muster up anything but 'small.' Yet I know that in Your hands, little is big. Even that which is very little. And therefore, I give You the very 'little' that I invested today because I know that You can make it so much more.

And that's what I want…more. I don't want a 'little' hope. I want a giant hope. An imposing hope. An impenetrable hope. A hope that can handily overcome everything that's thrown against it. A resilient hope. A bold and even audacious kind of hope. I want to live facing the testing, the disappointments, the heartbreaks, the betrayals, the setbacks, the pain with a durable and overcoming kind of hope. And tonight, that is my prayer.

I pray all of this in Jesus' Name. Amen.

A Thought to Prepare for Tomorrow

"I cannot begin to tell you how many times I have come to prayer broken far beyond any conceivable hope of repair. I have likewise come without anywhere to turn simply because, much like myself, everything around me lies broken beyond repair. And I cannot tell you how many times God has taken that which is broken and has used it to do what could never have done should any of that had been whole."

~ Craig D. Lounsbrough

From this day, I release to God...

Day 11

The Emptiness a Wasted Life

"Show me, LORD, my life's end and the number of my days; let me know how fleeting my life is. You have made my days a mere handbreadth; the span of my years is as nothing before you. Everyone is but a breath, even those who seem secure."

~Psalm 39:4-5

The tally of our years must have some identifiable total that gives us a sense that they were worthwhile and well spent. While we tend to squander our days and throw away the years, there is yet some deep and primordial sense that our lives must be made up of more than just the living of our lives. We must produce something that is greater than the sum total of our years and bigger than the sum total of ourselves. Our lives must matter more than simply having been lived 'expending' the resources around us rather than 'expanding' them so that others might be wonderfully enriched by our journey.

Some might call this legacy. Others much refer to it as purpose or calling or mission. However you might wish to conceptualize it, our lives must be greater than the sum total of whatever our years have been. We must leave more behind than what was here when we showed up. There must be a contribution of some sort that enhances life today but has the power and the reach to enhance a future that we will not be here to see. Such a reality is critical to our existence and central to our well-being.

Yet, many of us feel that our lives have utterly failed in this regard. We have wasted days, months, years, decades, and lifetimes. And this stark realization is accompanied by the suffocating feeling that the waste of time has been too great to reclaim with whatever time is left. That may be so. However, with God, "a day is like a thousand years, and a thousand years are like a day." Therefore, the only thing that can waste your life from this day forward is your attitude. God's waiting to do great things in you, and in His world He has all of the time in the world to do that.

"If we were to tally all of the potential that was never unleashed throughout the history of mankind, and if that tally was somehow held up in front of us, I would hope against all hope that it would horrify us to a point of such despair that we would be driven to insure that such a tragedy would never be given any shred of space anywhere in our own lives nor in the lives of any life that we might touch for the rest of our lives."

~ Craig D. Lounsbrough

Morning Prayer

Dear God:
If I could do it all over again, I would do it differently. Very differently. But I can't. I'm left with whatever it is that I've left myself with. This is where I am, and this is what I've got to work with. I can call it failure, or stupidity, or ignorance, or whatever word that I would like to use. But to whatever degree that I've done it, I have at some level wasted my life. I've discovered that I can waste a lot of things. But to waste life…how do I come back from that? How do I reconcile that? How do I live with what I can't fix?

So dear God, I need to know that You are not bound by the reckless and short-sighted choices that I've made. Neither are You bound by the time that I've squandered. All of the things that hold me the hostage of a life wasted have no hold on You.

You said that we should "number each of our days." Therefore, I hand You whatever days I have left. I hand You the resources that I still have, as scant and scarce as they might be. Whatever it is that I have not squandered I give to You. All of it. Take these things and make my life count. Make my life matter. May the years that are left overshadow the years that I've wasted. Use whatever I have left to make the world better today so that this same world will be far better tomorrow.

I pray all of this in Jesus's Name. Amen.

A Thought to Carry with Me Today

"I am made for a purpose. And it is worth expending everything that I have to find it, for I will waste everything that I have if I do not."

~ Craig D. Lounsbrough

Before this day, I release to God...

____

____

____

____

____

____

Evening Prayer

Dear God:
Today I thought about my life. I thought about how to do something with it that matters. And I don't mean something that matters for me. I mean something that matters for the people around me today, and those who will live here once I am gone.

Show me what that is. What do I invest my remaining years and resources in? What are You calling me to do, because whatever it is, I want to do it in ways that I would have never dreamt possible. I don't want to waste another minute, or another thought, or another opportunity. And I want to begin tomorrow by living that calling out. Right from the very moment that my feet hit the floor.

I pray all of this in Jesus' Name. Amen.

A Thought to Prepare for Tomorrow

"My purpose is waiting for me to step into it.
And I should do that the moment that I
step out of bed."

~ *Craig D. Lounsbrough*

From this day, I release to God...

Day 12

Fear of the Unknown

"The LORD himself goes before you and will be with you; he will never leave you nor forsake you. Do not be afraid; do not be discouraged."

~ Deuteronomy 31:8

The unknown. We don't know what it's carrying around inside of itself or what it's dragging along with it. We know that the unknown is out there, and we know that it's going to be headed our direction sooner or later. It's that thing that could come delivering some incredibly wonderful things to our lives. But it could also come packed full of some of the most horrible things imaginable that are set to detonate the very moment that they get within arm's reach of us.

But whatever it's carrying, good or bad…it's unknown. That means that there's no way to prepare. No way to know what to do, or what not to do.

The fact is, somewhere, at some time in each of our lives the unknown showed up and it blew us up. It came concealing an unexpected death, or divorce papers, or a child having overdosed, or a career wiped out, or a terminal illness, or an affair, or any one of the other ways that it's shown up. And when it did, the lights went out, the waters came up, hope evaporated, the future disappeared, depression knocked us flat, and life was no longer worth living.

And it is the horror of such moments that we associate with the unknown. We're not certain that we can take another hit like that. We're pretty convinced that we're only one loss away from a depression that we feel we will never crawl out of. One more death, one more lost relationship, one more child fighting for their lives, one more career setback, or terminal illness, or affair, or financial hit, and we're done. The fact that the unknown may show up with any one of these things is just too much.

"If you fall to your fears today, your tomorrow will fall before it had the chance to become your next today."

~ Craig D. Lounsbrough

Morning Prayer

Dear God:
There's a lot of unknowns out there. In fact, most of what's out there is unknown. The world's simply too big to know much of anything. And so, although I don't like it, I've got to live with a bunch of unknowns.

God, You know that a lot of those unknowns have been really bad for me. You know that some of them have scarred me deeply. I've got a big collection of wounds and some of those are still open and raw even today. I know that by its very nature life can be tough, and I know that it can be unfair. But I know that it's in our pain that we grow. I get that and I accept that. But still, why does it have to do the things to us that it does? Why the brutality? Why the cruelty? Why the viciousness? Why?

But then, why does so much of this hit us out of nowhere? Suddenly our lives spin off into some descending spiral that leaves us wishing that we were dead. That's how the unknown often shows up. And because that's the case, I hate it and I fear it.

But I know that the unknown is known to You. The Bibles says that "The Lord himself goes before [me] and will be with [me]." I know that whatever it is that life holds out there in the great unknown, You hold the unknown. And so Lord, help me to stand with You as You stand with me in facing the unknowns in my life. Then the unknown no longer needs to be known simply because You beat it before it even showed up.

I pray all of this in Jesus's Name. Amen.

A Thought to Carry with Me Today

"It doesn't matter what's coming at us. God defeated it before it ever left wherever it was coming from."

~ *Craig D. Lounsbrough*

Before this day, I release to God...

____

____

____

____

____

____

____

Evening Prayer

Dear God:
The unknown side-swiped me today. Again. And I know that it's likely that it will do the same thing tomorrow. But I know that nothing sideswipes You. Ever. The fact is, You sideswipe everything before it ever even gets a shot at me. And even that 'shot' is deflected by Your promise to walk with me through every storm that would dare cross the horizon of my life. Thank You for that.

It is my prayer that the unknown will become something that I refuse to fear. In fact, may I come to anticipate it; may even invite it. May I look forward to its arrival knowing that that's the very time and the very place that You begin to do some of Your most remarkable work. And so, I give You the unknown and whatever may come with it.

I pray all of this in Jesus' Name. Amen.

A Thought to Prepare for Tomorrow

"I don't need to understand the unknown because
I have a God for whom this thing was never
unknown to begin with. And because it has
always been known, I can take the fullest
comfort in the fact that the solution
to it has never not been known."

~ Craig D. Lounsbrough

From this day, I release to God...

Day 13

Refusing to Be the Fool

"Wise men store up knowledge, but the mouth of a fool invites ruin."
~ Proverbs 10:14

No matter where you go, you are certain to find a fool. The best that we can do in a world of fools is to make certain that we are not one of them.

Being a fool is the choice of an individual to live in blind pursuit of their lesser passions. It is a decision based on the belief that the easy road will meet their desires a manner that will cost them the least and deliver the most. The easy road is always a short road that abruptly dead ends, leaving the gullible among us to believe that it was not taken correctly, rather than realizing that it should never have been taken at all.

The fool is too foolish to see themselves as the fool. Therefore they repeat their mistakes, believing that the mistake would be believing that their choice was a mistake. And as failures are compounded by additional failures they trade insight for blame placing, adamantly declaring that life or circumstance or the economy or another person or bad luck or some sort of something else has caused the problem.

The only fool that we can control is the one that we hope to never become. That requires being thoughtful, basing decisions on sound principles, seeking out reliable resources, staying clear of cultural mandates that propagate trendy agendas, and making certain that decisions represent a good greater than ourselves.

Wisdom is the anthesis of the fool. If we proceed

with Godly wisdom we can be assured that the errors of the fool will not be our errors, and their consequences will never be visited upon us.

"Don't confuse stubbornness with determination, for the latter is driven by wisdom and the former is just driven."

~ Craig D. Lounsbrough

Morning Prayer

Dear God:
Whatever the fool is, keep me from being that. Keep me from being what I can so easily become. Keep me from the consequences of being a fool for all of the many reasons that I have been the fool in the past.

I know that I can so easily point the finger at others and make light of the consequences that their foolishness has resulted in. But doing that is the very foolishness that I say I am seeking to avoid. So, keep me from being foolish in the process of trying not to be the fool.

Your Word says that "If any of you lacks wisdom, you should ask God, who gives generously to all without finding fault, and it will be given to you." Give me Your wisdom and then grant me the wisdom to hold onto Your wisdom. It is Your wisdom that brought the whole of existence into being. It is Your wisdom that holds it all together. Without Your wisdom, my life would immediately fall into a chaos from which it would never recover. And having lived the brutality of such chaos, I am wise enough to know that it is not where I want to live any longer. So, grant me Your wisdom so that I might not live the consequences of the fool that I have too often been.

I pray all of this in Jesus's Name. Amen.

A Thought to Carry with Me Today

"Dear God, save me from the very 'me' that
I am unable to save myself from."

~ *Craig D. Lounsbrough*

Before this day, I release to God...

____

____

____

____

____

____

____

____

____

____

Evening Prayer

Dear God:
There were times today when I was the fool. And I lay here tonight feeling the consequences of those choices. I know that I was a fool for being the fool.

But I would rather learn from those choices rather than beat myself up for them, for that is being the fool that I say I don't want to be. So dear God, grant me Your wisdom. Give me what I don't have. But I would ask that You not just give it to me, for that would be far too easy. Give me the passion to pursue Your wisdom. Place within me the drive to raise myself up beyond where I have allowed myself to live and set me in an all-out pursuit of Your wisdom every morning and every night of every day.

And please know that it is not the consequences of being the fool that I seek to avoid, for that is far too shallow of a reason to pursue anything. Rather, help me pursue wisdom simply because it is the essence of Your character and I desire to embody more of that character.

I pray all of this in Jesus' Name. Amen.

A Thought to Prepare for Tomorrow

"I am wise enough to know that I don't wish to be the fool. And that in and of itself will help to keep me from being that very thing."

~ Craig D. Lounsbrough

From this day, I release to God...

Day 14

The Task of Forgiving Myself

"Brothers and sisters, I do not consider myself yet
to have taken hold of it. But one thing I do:
Forgetting what is behind and straining
toward what is ahead…"
~ Philippians 3:13

Forgiving ourselves is difficult because we have to straddle the dual (and entirely opposing) reality of being the culprit, while simultaneously being the one who graciously extends forgiveness. To embrace such a polarizing duality is extraordinarily difficult, to the degree that many live out their lives being entirely unable to forgive themselves.

Yet, being unable to forgive ourselves is debilitating. It effectively strands us at whatever the offense was. It halts our progression at the point and in the place where the transgression transpired. As such, whatever we did comes to define the whole of us as we are unable to see anything other than the offense and the conclusions that we have drawn about ourselves because of that offense.

Forgiving ourselves is about allowing ourselves to be ourselves. It's the determined refusal to allow the worst of us to define the best of us. It's the second chance that allows us to break whatever broke us in the first place. It's the key to every door that has slammed shut in a prison made up of walls that we built. And because we built them, we can also tear them down. That's what self-forgiveness does.

God has forgiven us. That's what He does. You cannot bring anything to the cross that it cannot wash as white as snow. So, no matter what you've done or how grievous it might be, no matter how much it haunts you, no matter how unforgivable you might believe it to be, God has forgiven you. And if He has actually done that, what can you possibly find to hold against yourself that's even remotely legitimate to hold against yourself?

"Forgiveness is telling ourselves that the
'wrong' that we did will not impede
the 'right' that we can do."
~ Craig D. Lounsbrough

Morning Prayer

Dear God:
Sometimes I can't even look in the mirror. Too often I am disgusted with myself beyond disgust. I can find absolutely no excuse for what I've done, no justification for the character traits that I've cultivated that resulted in this, and no room to defend anything about me that as some lesser person I might attempt to defend. I am my own judge and executioner, and I am brutal in ruthlessly carrying out the obligations of both.

I know that I am a prisoner to all of this. And I know that I hold the key, even though I am often unable to believe that I actually hold it. You said that, "If we confess our sins, [You] are faithful and just and will forgive our sins…" And if I somehow I do believe that You have granted me a gift that grand and that wildly liberating, I don't think myself worthy of having it. This prison should be my lot. I deserve this life. I am where I belong. But that is the voice of unforgiveness that I wish to silence. Today.

I know that staying where I am will rob me of everything that You wish me to know, to have, and to do. It is the unnecessary prison of my own guilt. The illegitimate cell, despite how legitimate I believe it to be. So dear God, help me to forgive myself in just the same manner that You have forgiven me.

I pray all of this in Jesus's Name. Amen.

A Thought to Carry with Me Today

"Forgiveness brilliantly rewrites the script that we've penned to process the pain and betrayal of our histories. And while such a rewrite does not change history itself, it changes everything about our history."

~ Craig D. Lounsbrough

Before this day, I release to God...

___

___

___

___

___

___

___

___

___

___

Evening Prayer

Dear God:
Tonight I forgive myself for not forgiving myself. I forgive myself for those that I've hurt. Those who I've betrayed. Those who I've walked away from at their time of need. I forgive myself for the lies, for the deceit, for the cowardice that resulted in awful decisions, and for all of the things that are contrary to Your will for my life.

But I know that forgiveness demands change. It demands that things be different. That I learn and grow from what I've done in order to make certain that I don't do those things again. And I would much rather focus on changing my life instead of focusing on all of the things that I've done to destroy my life. Forgiving myself is the first (and necessary) step toward that goal. Please help me to do exactly that.

I pray all of this in Jesus' Name. Amen.

A Thought to Prepare for Tomorrow

"Forgiveness allows the burdens that we carry to become the histories that we forget."

~ Craig D. Lounsbrough

From this day, I release to God...

Day 15

Dealing With Aging Parents

"Honor your father and your mother, so that you
may live long in the land the LORD
your God is giving you."

~ Exodus 20:12

Aging is not a journey taken in isolation. It is a joint journey undertaken by every human being on the face of the earth. Some are behind us in this journey. Some are right alongside of us. And others, like our parents, are ahead of us.

Our parents are where we are going. They are the future looking us in the face. Take away the years that separate us from them and suddenly we are them and they are us.

As our parents age, our roles reverse. We become increasingly independent. They become increasingly dependent. Our abilities expand. Theirs dwindle. We have enough future in front of us to talk about it, while the future for them is now history passed…so that is what they talk about. The divide deepens over time, leaving both with a shared history, but with a present that is shared largely by time and far less by experience.

The goal of an aging parent is to end well. Not avoid the ending, for that's a waste of whatever time their final days afford them. It is an acknowledgement of time evaporating, with the concurrent commitment of making this time as rich as their condition will permit. It is to bring to a culmination what life has been, to celebrate the good, to grieve the past where appropriate, to forgive where needed, and share this time of twilight with a younger generation that will carry pieces of it forward into their own future. If we, as the children of these parents can provide our parents the resources to age in just such a manner as this, we will have been a blessing to them, they a blessing to us, and we will be infinitely better prepared when this time arrives in our own lives.

"It's not the specter of aging that haunts me. Rather, it's the far greater fear of having aged and having nothing to show for the aging."

~ Craig D. Lounsbrough

Morning Prayer

Dear God:
Sin ages us. It steals that which was meant to be forever and grinds it down to an existence that evaporates before our very eyes. Life is shorter than we think it is, and it slips away faster than what we had anticipated even by our most realistic estimates. "[We] are but a mist that appears for a little while and then vanishes."

Dear God, I know that the end will arrive much sooner than I had anticipated. And as I watch aging parents, that end is but a few steps away. My prayer for them is that You would give them whatever they need at this time…in abundance. If they need to heal in some way, heal them. If they carry some sort of unforgiveness, help them to forgive. If they're burdened with regret, release them from whatever that is. If there's unresolved trauma, some loss that they've yet to let go of, a wound that's still bleeding, a relationship that remains broken, heal them from all of these things.

May these twilight years (or days if that be the case), be filled with whatever they need to be filled with in order to close out this parents' life in a manner rich, healed, accomplished, and genuinely appreciated.

I pray all of this in Jesus's Name. Amen.

A Thought to Carry with Me Today

"I believe that I would find it a nightmare of the most nightmarish sort to face my dying day suddenly realizing that I had died long before this day arrived. Therefore, I need to live now so that dying can wait until later."

~ Craig D. Lounsbrough

Before this day, I release to God...

____

____

____

____

____

____

____

____

____

Evening Prayer

Dear God:
I am now one day older. That means that I am one day closer to the day when my life will end. Everyone on the planet faces the same reality that I do. The clocks ticks just the same for all of us.

But for some, the days are fewer. That doesn't necessarily make every day more precious, as each day is precious no matter what our age. But for those with only a handful of them left, there may be something a bit more precious about them. And so, I would ask You to bless these aging parents with whatever they might need in order to live out these last moments completely wrapped in a sturdy sense of peace and comfort. And I would like to ask you that as I age, You would shape my life so that when I arrive at that place in time I too will be blessed with those very same things.

I pray all of this in Jesus' Name. Amen.

A Thought to Prepare for Tomorrow

"It is the geese plying the graying skies of autumn in floating V-formations on a rendezvous with southern horizons that gives me the greatest pause. For my life is rarely raised to the calls of life on the wing that beg me to rise up and lay hold of distant horizons in search of a season being birthed out of the one now dying. For to stay here in a season now expired is to die along with it, and despite the fact that I had died many times, I must never forget that I can still fly."

~ Craig D. Lounsbrough

From this day, I release to God...

Day 16

Letting Go of the Loved Ones Who Hurt Us

"Many have become my enemies without cause,
those who hate me without reason are numerous.
Those who repay my good with evil lodge
accusations against me, though I seek
only to do what is good."
~ Psalm 38:19-20

Wounds can be healed, even the deepest kind. Forgiveness is never short on its ability to overcome the greatest abuses imaginable, even though such forgiveness may take a great deal of time, a softening of our own hearts, and a large margin of discomfort. Restoration is never beyond our reach, nor any relationship beyond recovery.

Yet, there are those who will not permit healing. They feel the need to nurse a grudge, cling to a perceived offense, refuse compromise, work to leverage some sort of revenge, or use their pain to enhance ours as some sort of righteous retribution.

Sometimes those whom we love the most are the ones that stand in the way of that love. Sometimes the very people for whom we would stand in defense of (or possibly die for) stand in direct opposition to us. And despite the fact that restoration stands at the ready, at times we have no alternative but to walk away from the very person who we are desperate to walk towards.

Whether this is a sibling, a spouse, a parent, a lifelong friend, a comrade who walked with us through any one of life's battles, or someone else. Too often we have to let go of the person who we love because they refuse to love us. The sadness in it all is the reality that this need not be. The loss is a choice, not a destiny. Yet, even though we are forced to walk away, our prayers can continue to walk with them. We may be forced to say "goodbye," but our prayers can be a constant "hello."

"I can always be present through the prayers that I pray for those who no longer wish me to be present."
~ Craig D. Lounsbrough

Morning Prayer

Dear God:
My heart is a bit empty this morning. It's the kind of empty that especially empty because it doesn't need to be empty. I am facing the choice of a loved one to no longer love me. Or maybe they do love me, but not enough to see past the pain that sits squarely in the middle of our relationship. I feel what David felt when he wrote, "Even my close friend, whom I trusted, he who shared by bread, has lifted up his heel against me." I'm living those words this morning.

If there is something that I need to do that I have not yet done, let me know what the might be. If I have done all that I can, if I have exhausted the resources available to me to heal this, and if anything further would be damaging, let me see that and allow me to rest in it so that I might have some thread of peace in my loss.

Finally, I know that I have to walk away, but I know that my prayers do not. I only need to come before You and You are instantly with them. And so, dear God, I pray for them. I pray for their healing. I pray that You would go with them since I cannot. I pray that You would shield them, speak to them, and be to them what I can no longer be.

I pray all of this in Jesus's Name. Amen.

A Thought to Carry with Me Today

"To leave someone because their choices demand that we do so is not to give up on them. For even though I may never see them again, dear God You see them every minute of every day. And in the seeing, I ask that You see what I could not, and be what I cannot."

~ Craig D. Lounsbrough

Before this day, I release to God...

Evening Prayer

Dear God:
I'm going to bed with a hole in my heart. And I know that this hole will always be there. But I also know that it will heal and the day will come when the pain will be more of a memory than a reality. I really wouldn't want to lose the hole anyway, because I never want to forget the person who left that place in my heart as sometimes forgetting can be the biggest loss of all.

Tonight I pray less for me and more for them. I know that they carry their own pain, their disappointments, the triggers that incite them to retreat, the defense mechanisms that rise to protect them from their own wounds. And I ask that You move to heal them and encourage them in whatever way that needs that done tonight, tomorrow, and every tomorrow after that.

I pray all of this in Jesus' Name. Amen.

A Thought to Prepare for Tomorrow

"Sometimes a goodbye is a necessary part of a
larger journey that we do not understand.
And at times, if the goodbye doesn't
happen the next hello won't either."

~ Craig D. Lounsbrough

From this day, I release to God...

Day 17

Praying for Those Who Have Left Their Faith

"Do your best to come to me quickly, for Demas, because he loved this world, has deserted me and has gone to Thessalonica."

~ 2 Timothy 4:9-10

Great things demand great things of us. Lesser things demand the abandonment of great things by masquerading as great things themselves, for great things expose lesser things as putrid, pathetic, and undesirable. Therefore, lesser things must lead us to believe that the great things that we might pursue are themselves masquerading as something that they are not.

Lesser things come with a hidden but entirely astronomical cost that exceeds whatever price we might incur in pursuing great things. And that cost comes in opportunities blatantly squandered, dreams thoughtlessly gutted, goals rendered passive, vision blinded, healing forfeited, and life compromised to lifeless apathy.

God calls us to great things. That's the nature of what He does. We are not called to passivity or the lie of lesser things. The call of God is a holy calling that exceeds the standards held by the world, and it eclipses the ability of men to accomplish that calling without the God who's done the calling. Yet, in the press of life with its escalating demands, searing losses, increasing uncertainty, betrayals of all sorts, and the confusion of a culture gone sideways, some people come to believe that the lesser things liberally propagated by the world are actually the greater things.

And therefore, they fall to the lesser things of the world and they fall away from the greater things once embodied in their faith. They opt for a world of lesser things that will render them lesser people. The loss of faith in something better can make everything better slip away and we are left watching a friend or a spouse or a child walk into a darkness born of a dark choice driven by a world of lesser things.

"If we believe that the rational for betraying God could ever justify the betrayal itself, we have shown that we possess the ability to betray anything, including ourselves."
~ Craig D. Lounsbrough

Morning Prayer

Dear God:
Someone walked away from You today. Someone, somewhere decided that walking with You was inferior to walking with lesser things. And in walking away from You, they walked into a darkness that presented itself as light. And there is nothing darker than a darkness that pretends to be light.

But I know that even though they may walk away, You do not. You have committed Yourself to a relentless hunt for that one "lost sheep." I know that You are wherever they go. I know that You will speak to them in whatever manner their situation demands. I know that You will press against the darkness and You will speak into the betrayal that they have engaged in. I know that Your word will not fall flat, Your truth will set itself in front of them again and again, and that You will seek the "lost sheep" into whatever wilderness they may wander.

And so, dear God, I ask You to do all of those things and more. I ask You to be relentless in Your pursuit of a soul gone astray. And I ask You that You might grant me the opportunity to be part of bringing them back.

I pray all of this in Jesus's Name. Amen.

A Thought to Carry with Me Today

"To fight for greater things is the essence of our humanity. Therefore, to fall to the skepticism of those for whom the essence of the fight is lost is to lose the greater fight for the essence of our humanity."

~ *Craig D. Lounsbrough*

Before this day, I release to God...

___

___

___

___

___

___

___

___

___

Evening Prayer

Dear God:
Today someone walked away. But I am also confident that today someone walked back. Today there was a victory that reminds me that a defeat is more of an attitude than a reality.

Therefore, I pray for the ones who came home today. I pray that their journey back to You brought a depth and a maturation to their lives that will forever strengthen their faith and embolden their testimony.

And for those who walked away, make their journey difficult. Render the road unexpectedly rugged. Crush the false ideals and arrogant lies that prompted their departure in the first place. Do so to the point that they ultimately return to You with a fresh and potent commitment that will never flag nor fail.

I pray all of this in Jesus' Name. Amen.

A Thought to Prepare for Tomorrow

"It's understanding that nothing is ever lost until
we think that it is. And we must remember
that no thought of ours has the power
to make something lost that is not."

~ Craig D. Lounsbrough

From this day, I release to God...

Day 18

Praying for Leaders

"Not many of you should become teachers, my fellow believers, because you know that we who teach will be judged more strictly."
~ James 3:1

It is extremely difficult to separate a deep sense of distrust from the concept of leadership. Sadly, that distrust is rightfully rooted in the abuse, incompetence, and mismanagement of many in leadership today. That is not to say that all leaders function in this manner as that would be as much an abuse of the definition of leadership as the abuses perpetrated by some in leadership themselves.

An essential part of our prayer life is to cultivate a vigorous conviction to pray for those in leadership rather than fall prey to some sense of discouragement or apathy or anger in light of the abuses of leadership that constantly bombard us. While we must raise up those who abuse the trust of leadership, we must also pray for those that serve rightly that they would be strengthened in their convictions, shielded from the criticisms that integrity can invite, and be used to correctly lead those who lead abusively.

To pray for a leader is not to pray for an agenda with which we disagree, or to bless a platform that is ethically impoverished. To pray for leaders is to petition the Leader of all leaders to decisively intersect these lives in whatever way that He chooses to do so. It is to bring the greatest Leader of all into the middle of all that is evil so that He might crush it, and to put an invincible hedge around all that is good in order to enlarge it.

It may be that not praying for leaders is the reason that we have so many of the destructive leaders that we have today. And it may well be that we radically change the landscape of leadership by aggressively calling God Himself into that very landscape.

> "To lead for glory or gain is to neither lead nor follow. Rather, it is to destroy."
> ~ *Craig D. Lounsbrough*

Morning Prayer

Dear God:
I know that it is less about the position of leadership itself, and more about the person who fills it. It's about possessing a Godly value system that is fixed sufficiently to overcome any system that would come against it, even the system that's being led. It's about standing on timeless principles every time and at all times. It's about leading on behalf of those that one is leading, not on our own behalf. And I know that in some capacity I will find myself leading today. It might be of little note and brief, or it might be deeply impacting and protracted. In whatever way that I do that today, may I lead holding tightly to these principles despite the cost of doing so.

But I pray for those in leadership positions whatever and wherever those might be. In particular I pray for those who exercise direct leadership over me. Guide them, Infuse them with wisdom. If their path is in error, set it right. If they are bending to questionable agendas, stand them straight. If they are entertaining a stance of compromise, force them out of the entertainment business. Grant them wisdom. Give them discernment. Embolden them for that which is right and render them deeply averse to all that is wrong for "you test the heart and are pleased with integrity." May all of those in leadership today understand that the greatest accomplishment in any position of leadership is to pass this test.

I pray all of this in Jesus's Name. Amen.

A Thought to Carry with Me Today

"A great leader is someone who first
mastered the art of following."
~ *Craig D. Lounsbrough*

Before this day, I release to God...

Evening Prayer

Dear God:
Today leaders made all kinds of decision. Many were good and right. Many were not. My prayer would be that those who made the 'good and right' decisions be blessed and their work be fruitful and multiply. May those who did not make such decisions find themselves vexed by their choices and standing awash in the consequences of those choices. And may this happen not to hurt them or deliver some sort of punishment. Rather, may it happen to transform them and to do so profoundly.

And I pray that as I led in whatever capacity that I led today that I did so in a manner that advanced those that I led, even if it did not advance me. May the lives around me be blessed as I lead them in whatever way that You have call me to lead them.

I pray all of this in Jesus' Name. Amen.

A Thought to Prepare for Tomorrow

"A 'good' leader recognizes that they have been granted the uncommon experience of leading common men. A 'great' leader recognizes that of all men, they are likely the most common."

~ Craig D. Lounsbrough

From this day, I release to God...

Day 19

Effectively Praying for Our Children

"Train up a child in the way he should go; even when he is old he will not depart from it."
~ Proverbs 22:6

Children are the next generation under construction. Who we were will be boldly illustrated in whatever it is that they became. They are what will be left of us in a generation that we will not be a part of.

As we take on this unprecedented task, we would be wise to understand the world into which they are beginning to venture and within which they will eventually launch for the remainder of their lives. The challenges are massive. The enemies are relentless. The pitfalls are unforgiving, and the resources for their own destruction are ever-present.

The time that we have to shape a human being is limited to a mere handful years that seem far too brief to do the job effectively. Such brevity speaks to the fact that we must pour the fullness of our lives into our children for the brief span that we have them.

Given that brevity, prayer is the most durable gift that we can give them. Prayer is not bound to the limitations of the time to which we are bound. It will extend into a future that lays beyond our own existence, leaving with them a piece of us that forever goes beyond us. It sets us squarely in situations where we are not, grants them protection we cannot, and guides them in situations where our voice is not.

Praying for our children is to extend our lives into the life of someone who will be living out their lives in a time and place that we will never see. Yet, our prayers will not only see that place, they will shape it.

"Each and every day take the time to tell your children the great people that they are so that they don't grow up living each and every day thinking they're the bad people that they're not."

~ Craig D. Lounsbrough

Morning Prayer

Dear God:
You have set before our children a world that is taking shape at the same time that they are taking shape. The challenges today are great, likely greater than any other time in history. And it is this future that we will be sending these children into.

This morning I pray for all children as each one is "a heritage from the Lord." I pray for the ones I have, but also the ones that I don't. I pray for children who today find themselves in impoverished neighborhoods being enslaved by poverty and the lack of hope that impoverishment feeds. I pray for children of broken families who are trying to navigate an existence that they did not create and do not understand. I pray for children who have been abused and who are already beset with a trauma that haunts them at every turn. I pray for children who find nothing good in themselves, who are marginalized by society and rejected by their peer group. This morning I pray for children who have contemplated how to take their lives before even figuring out how to live their lives. Dear God, I pray for every child in every household of every nation. Bless the children Father!

I pray all of this in Jesus's Name. Amen.

A Thought to Carry with Me Today

"While your children are only born once, the process of birthing something into them happens every day thereafter."

~ Craig D. Lounsbrough

Before this day, I release to God...

____

____

____

____

____

____

____

____

____

____

Evening Prayer

Dear God:
Every child is now a day older. Every child now lives with the experience of yet another day behind them. Whatever their day has been and whatever these twenty-four hours have held for them, I pray that it will build them and not destroy them. I pray that the worst that any child experienced today will be used to strengthen them rather than cripple them, grant them hope rather than rob them of it, bring them a peace that outlasts any fear, and the anticipation of a new tomorrow that crushes any dread about what lays before them.

Be with the children, Father. Walk with them. Hold them. Shield them. Lift them. Love them. Discipline them for a greater good, encourage them so that they might achieve all that is good, and love them because they are good.

I pray all of this in Jesus' Name. Amen.

A Thought to Prepare for Tomorrow

"On every trip back to the Midwest, I step aside from my schedule and visit my parent's graves. And with trimmers in hand I kneel down and I cut back the intruding grasses and occasional weed that has edged up against their headstones. It is not in grief that I do this, but in the fondest recollection. The tears that often visit me there are those of joy; that God had thought enough of me to bless me with parent's rich in love, ever bound by sacrifice, and sturdy in faith despite the nature of the adversities that so often beset them. And as I leave their graves and head back to the pressing demands of my world, I depart with the commitment to live my life in a manner that my children will find no grief at my grave, but joy in knowing that God chose me for them."

~ Craig D. Lounsbrough

From this day, I release to God...

Day 20

Dealing With the Darkness of Depression

"The Lord himself goes before you and will be with you; he will never leave you nor forsake you. Do not be afraid; do not be discouraged."
~ Deuteronomy 31:8

Sometimes the difficulties in life overwhelm the resources that we have to cope with them. The perpetual onslaught of disappointments, losses, betrayals, unexpected setbacks, incessant demands, and problems which repeatedly elude any solutions that we bring to them eventually swamps us. Subsequently, we end up with a depression that we can't fight because we're exhausted from fighting all of the other things that brought us to this point of depression.

It's not that we don't 'fight the good fight.' It's just that the fight is often bigger than our resources to fight it. We know that life comes with battles, and we're aware that challenges are a natural part of our existence. But at times our resources are decisively overwhelmed and our ability to cope is diminished or rendered altogether absent.

Some depression is genetic. Most is situational. Depression occurs when we become engulfed in a level sadness that undermines our ability to function adequately. Oddly enough, depression is frequently compounded less by the situation that caused it and more by the fact that we have depression in the first place. Depression can also be exacerbated by this haunting fear that it may deepen right at the time in our lives when our emotional resources have already been spent attempting to manage what depression we already have.

We would be wise to remember that a large part of our depression is rooted in how we choose to think about our lives and our circumstances. Therefore, if we bring the power of prayer and the fresh hope that prayer embodies to bear on the realities in our lives, we can begin the process of overcoming our depression by changing how we think about it because we've included God in it.

"Darkness is a sad and often terrible part of this existence, but it never defines this existence."

~ Craig D. Lounsbrough

Morning Prayer

Dear God:
I feel very heavy, and the heaviness that I feel seems dark and cold. These feelings have immobilized me despite the fact that I've tried to fight them as best I can. I have to say that they've left me feeling worn and helpless.

It's just that life got hard. The disappointments have been crushing when I think about them. The pain has gone on for so long that all of it just grinds me down. Life has become something that I have to endure because I've come to a place where I'm finding it hard (and at times impossible) to live with any kind of enthusiasm or joy. And I've come to realize that these attitudes have become my norm. They've become my expectation of what life is going to be for me. From where I'm sitting, I can't see anything else in front of me other than this.

I know that this is not Your intent for me. This is not the way that You want me to live my life. You tell us to "cast all of [our] anxiety on [you]." I know that You have more for me and that's why I'm coming to You tonight. I'm asking You for more than this dark existence that I can't shake myself free of. I'm asking You to strengthen me while I'm in the middle of this, and then I'm asking You to free me from it.

I pray all of this in Jesus's Name. Amen.

A Thought to Carry with Me Today

"With God, the word 'impossible' is itself impossible."

~ Craig D. Lounsbrough

Before this day, I release to God…

____

____

____

____

____

____

____

____

____

____

Evening Prayer

Dear God:
I got through the day. Even saying that makes me sad, but it's how I feel. And I know that You were a huge part of getting me through this day.

But I don't want to just 'get through the day.' I want to live through the day. I want to celebrate the day. I want to rejoice in the day and live out those moments that give me a hope for the next day. I guess I'm saying that I want to live in a way that I haven't lived for a really long time.

So dear God, pull away the layers of depression that suffocate my heart, give me a hope greater than the darkness, a peace greater than the turmoil, a confidence greater than the challenges, and freedom from everything that would bind me.

I pray all of this in Jesus' Name. Amen.

A Thought to Prepare for Tomorrow

"The worst of it is that while we continue to sink deeper into the muck and mire that we've created, in the very descent itself we ignorantly declare that in reality we are rising. And until desperation has crippled us sufficiently to confess the lie that we are lifting ourselves out of this mess, and until the panic of utter hopelessness has driven us to completely surrender all of the pathetic contrivances that we've fashioned that have put us there, we will never realize that God has readied solid ground that stands but a single step away."

~ *Craig D. Lounsbrough*

From this day, I release to God...

Day 21

Dealing With Anxiety

"Casting all your anxieties on him,
because he cares for you."
~ 1 Peter 5:7

Worry. If you look at the world today, it's not all that hard to figure out why so many people are quite literally plagued with worry. However, the core of our worry is largely centered on our feeling that we have no ability to manage or impact that which worries us. We feel that we are facing difficulties, dangers, and daunting issues that we cannot control, much less influence in any constructive manner. In some sense we feel that we are along for a ride that is ultimately going to end in some terribly catastrophic manner.

Therefore we feel frighteningly ill at ease. We feel intensely vulnerable. We are consistently overwhelmed with a terrifying sense of helplessness. We sense that we are being held unwitting captives to a deteriorating financial situation, an unwanted divorce, an unforgiving addiction, a rotting self-esteem, a disintegrating culture, or any number of perilous dynamics that exceed whatever degree of influence that we might bring to them. Our experience is often accentuated by the very real realities that those who do possess some degree of power frequently exercise that power in a way that only serves to make these dynamics worse because that somehow serves their agenda.

Likely the greatest anxiety of all is to be left alone in our anxiety. On one side we have the issues that torment us. On the other side are those that thrust those issues into our lives. And muddling somewhere in the mix there are those who took advantage of our vulnerabilities and deepened our anxiety by stepping in and claiming that they could heal it when their intent was to take advantage of it.

But above it all is the God Who wants to remove both sides and yank out the middle right along with all of it. This God wishes to fill us with a "[peace] which transcends all understanding" regardless of the immensity, intensity, or hopelessness of that which we face. God is an anxiety killer, and He stands ready to do that for us.

"Anxiety is the absence of peace,
not the elimination of it."

~ *Craig D. Lounsbrough*

Morning Prayer

Dear God:
My heart is pounding right now. I can feel the tension engulfing me even as I'm praying this. I'm not certain that I had many moments today where I felt any other way. The fact is, I really can't recall many moments where I experienced a reasonable peace at all. And if I did, it didn't last for long. My life has too often been hijacked by an anxiety that seems to stalk me wherever I go.

You said that You "know the plans that You have for me…" I know that anxiety is not Your plan for me, or anyone else for that matter. But I also know that anxiety quite clearly illustrates my inability to trust

You like I should. And I confess that fact, even though the confession of it makes me anxious as well.

Give me a faith that is bigger than my anxiety because I can't seem to find a faith that big, much less rest in it. Give me a confidence in You that will stand strong even when the world throws the worst of itself at me. I am exhausted by my anxiety. But more than that, I am tired of not giving it all to You and trusting that You are big enough to wrestle my greatest fears into complete submission. That is what I want because I know that is what You wish to give me.

I pray all of this in Jesus's Name. Amen.

A Thought to Carry with Me Today

"It would behoove me to realize that I can't build a stronghold of any kind. Rather, I can only find one. And unless the stronghold that I find is God, everything that I fear will have a 'strong hold' on me."

~ Craig D. Lounsbrough

Before this day, I release to God...

____

____

____

____

____

____

____

____

____

____

Evening Prayer

Dear God:
I faced the world again today. There were moments when I reigned in my anxiety and faced it fairly well, and there were moments when I did not. There were moments when I avoided what I shouldn't have avoided because the anxiety was too much, and there were moments when I told myself that my anxiety was not an excuse to avoid what I needed to face. And so, in whatever way I did it, I faced it.

But I want to live in a way that I can face whatever anxiety puts in my face. I want to be bold. And if I can't be bold, I want to press against my anxiety until I am. So, please give me what I need to do that. And if You see fit to rid me of my anxiety, I would ask that I always remember that no anxiety is greater than Your ability to free me of it.

I pray all of this in Jesus' Name. Amen.

A Thought to Prepare for Tomorrow

"If you fall to your fears today, your tomorrow
will fall before it had the chance to
become your next today."

~ Craig D. Lounsbrough

From this day, I release to God...

Day 22

Coping With Infidelity

"Marriage should be honored by all, and the marriage bed kept pure, for God will judge the adulterer and all the sexually immoral."
~ Hebrews 13:4

We all make commitments. We decide that something has sufficient value for us to give our lives over to it. We determine that the value of this thing to us or to others is worthy of the demands that it would make of us. And so, we commit.

But in time the value of this thing wanes. Or something of greater value presents itself to us. Or we've moved into a different phase of life where our goals, or our values, or our priorities have shifted. It is our sense that times are different, and as such what was worthwhile before is not.

The commitments that we made don't have the weight anymore. The determination to stand behind them flags, and we excuse ourselves from our duty to fulfill our promises. We do these things, or we find them happening to us.

And likely the most devastating place that this happens is in our marriages. A commitment for life becomes a commitment to self. "To death do us part," becomes a matter of convenience or preference. Someone else is more interesting, or new, or exciting, or younger. It's a fresh start with someone else's old problems.

Suddenly, a marriage is over because the thought of being with someone else overrode the commitment to another. A fantasy is constructed around someone else because the reality of facing the inevitable challenges of life in a committed relationship has become unappealing. A marriage is betrayed, a family destroyed, a future wrecked, and lives tossed aside as if used refuse.

"No betrayal is so big that God's commitment to us and presence within us is not bigger."

~ *Craig D. Lounsbrough*

5

Morning Prayer

Dear God:
I am alone and I am not supposed to be. I built a life based on the security of a commitment. And that commitment was broken. It was abandoned. It was cast aside in favor of another person and another life. And suddenly, nothing is the same.

The world is an uncertain place. And it is the people within it that are the largest contributors to that sad reality. I know that we all have those tendencies with us. I know that I have them within me. I can be just as shallow and self-serving as anybody else. And in the middle of the infidelity that I've experienced, I know that the roots of that kind of behavior sit dormant in me.

And so, heal the pain and loss within me. Heal the loss of trust that I now feel. Give me the wisdom to create a new life despite the fact that I prefer the old one. Grant me a new day and fresh opportunities that I can't see from this dark place that I'm sitting in.

But also, heal the one that betrayed me. There is no excuse for betrayal. But I also know that it arises from their pain as well. Heal them while You heal me, for it is in praying for the healing of another that I heal as well.

I pray all of this in Jesus's Name. Amen.

A Thought to Carry with Me Today

"Forgiveness brilliantly rewrites the script that we've penned to process the pain and betrayal of our histories. And while such a rewrite does not change history itself, it changes everything about our history."

~ *Craig D. Lounsbrough*

Before this day, I release to God...

____

____

____

____

____

____

____

____

____

____

Evening Prayer

Dear God:
The affair haunted me at times today. I found myself asking if I was good enough, or if I had enough to offer another, or if I wasn't as invested in the marriage as I should have been, or if I made a mistake getting married at all. That stuff rolled through my head today as it does every day.

I want to process what I need to process, but I want to rid myself of the pain at the same time so that I no longer have to process it. I don't want my life to be defined by the choices of another. I don't want to hand them that much power. Therefore, heal me so that my life might be defined by what You've done in it, not what someone else did to it.

I pray all of this in Jesus' Name. Amen.

A Thought to Prepare for Tomorrow

"So might it be that whatever I've lost in my life is what creates the space for whatever I've yet to gain in my life. Therefore, without loss I am without gain."

~ *Craig D. Lounsbrough*

From this day, I release to God...

Day 23

Creating a Work/Life Balance

"Be very careful, then, how you live—not as unwise but as wise, making the most of every opportunity, because the days are evil."
~ Ephesians 5:15

We might live conscious of the day, but not necessarily of 'the days.' We know that life is limited, but we don't seem to project that understanding out beyond the day that we're currently pressing through. We live counting the hours because we're living those right now. But we don't seem to count the weeks, or the months, or the years, or the decades because those don't reflect the realities of the moment that we are currently wrestling with or working through.

We tend to parcel out our resources based on the rubric of a single day verses the span of a lifetime. The urgency of what stands immediately in front of us consumes our ability to focus on the future which also stands in front of us. The unending rush of the moment drives our decisions, versus being driven by the vision of where we want this collection of moments and decisions to take us.

This often manifests itself in a work/life balance that is misaligned and skewed. It becomes heavily reactionary and limited in both focus and vision. We tend toward selfish gain, the demands of a career, mounting bills, the untarnished image that we wish to project, or the mad rush for security in whatever way we view security. It's about the preferences of the day rather than a vision for tomorrow.

And the result is a life expended madly chasing that which can never be caught and thereby wasting days that can never be reclaimed. And if perchance we could catch these things, we would find ourselves as empty as we were before we ever set off in pursuit of them. In end, imbalance become our end.

"The ledger of my life can lean heavy with a prolific array of stellar investments, yet in the tallying I would be wise to remember that an investment that is not of God will leave a zero balance on the ledger of life no matter how many ways I try to add it up."

~ Craig D. Lounsbrough

Morning Prayer

Dear God:
My imbalance is obvious. I don't like to admit that to You. I don't even like hearing myself say it to myself. But I am imbalanced. However, imbalance is not terminal.

I am imbalanced because of the selfish and less than wise choices that I have made. My greed gets the better of me. The desire for recognition steals away my common sense. The fear of failure dogs my steps and nips at my heels. The pressures of a misguided culture that I fall prey to. All of that and more causes me to make poor choices and indefensible decisions. And as such, I am out of balance.

And so, put me back in balance…if I ever was in balance in the first place. Help me to embrace Biblical principles and hold tight to the priorities that emerge from those principles for they are the embodiment of balance. Whatever I do, I want to "work at it with all [my] heart, as working for [You]." That is balance in the making and balance for the keeping. God, grant me this balance for the balance of my life.

I pray all of this in Jesus's Name. Amen.

A Thought to Carry with Me Today

"In the thoughtlessness of my incessant hurry, I have made God an 'addendum in' my life verses the 'agenda of' my life. And what I need to hurry up and realize is that with these priorities positioned as such, what I am hurrying to is my own demise."

~ Craig D. Lounsbrough

Before this day, I release to God...

____

____

____

____

____

____

____

____

____

Evening Prayer

Dear God:
Today I worked to bring balance to my imbalance. I think that in some ways I did that well. In others, I did not. But I know that praying this prayer itself and talking with You in the way that I'm talking to You right now helps bring that balance.

Balance is hard. It means breaking old patterns of behavior. It means deciding to leave behind things that I've come to cherish in order to embrace what You cherish. It means running against the cultural current and being willing to be seen as odd, outdated, or politically incorrect, or simply stupid. But you know, I don't care. I want Your balance in my life for every day that I have to live life.

I pray all of this in Jesus' Name. Amen.

A Thought to Prepare for Tomorrow

"I can work on changing what I've become. Or I can stop engaging in the things that have made me become the person I'm trying to change. And if I'm not serious about the latter, I can forget the former."

~ Craig D. Lounsbrough

From this day, I release to God...

Day 24

Dealing With Trauma

"He will cover you with his feathers, and under his wings you will find refuge; his faithfulness will be your shield and rampart. You will not fear the terror of night, nor the arrow that flies by day, nor the pestilence that stalks in the darkness, nor the plague that destroys at midday."
~ Psalm 91:4-6

Life can be brutal. We have this inherent sense that it should not be that way. But it is. There's a stubborn thread running deep within us that's an intimate throwback to a perfect time in a perfect garden for which we were perfectly suited. And while there's a future that stands in front us where that perfection will be perfectly restored, we currently live in a place and in a time where that perfection is a promised hope but not a current reality.

Therefore, bad things happen. Terrible things. Horrific things. Things that rip the foundations of our lives apart and alter the entire trajectory of our existence. We're left with memories that we can't shake, fears that we can't outrun, nightmares that stalk our sleep, and hope that remains frustratingly elusive despite how frantic the search.

There are times when the gravity of what has pummeled us is so great that time doesn't heal it, methods of self-medication fail to numb it, prayers don't seem to dent it, comforting words can't soften it, and an entire library of self-help books have neither the wisdom nor the power to soothe any part of it.

Yes…life can be brutal. But that doesn't relegate us to being a victim. Healing takes the time that we don't want to give it. But if we do, we will soon discover that the growth embedded in our devastation has the remarkable capacity to exceed the pain that spawned it. Pain is painful. Yet, there is immense opportunity in the worst of pain.

"Trauma buries me. But prayer has a huge shovel."

~ Craig D. Lounsbrough

Morning Prayer

Dear God:
I have memories within me that haunt me. Sometimes all that I have to do is close my eyes and the images are playing out right in front of me like I'm living them all over again. I hear a song, or read something, or someone makes a random comment and I'm right back in the middle of the very things that haunt my heart.

It seems that these memories are now part of my existence. They seem to be an immovable thread that cannot be untangled or removed. I am helpless to get rid of them. Sometimes I feel doomed to a life defined by the pain that I never asked for.

But I come to You to heal me. These moments do not need to define me. They don't need to haunt me, or shame me, or fill me with fear, or drive me to self-hatred, or throw me into depression. You can free me of that. You said, "whoever listens to me will dwell secure and will be at ease, without dread of disaster." Right how I claim the fact that You are my liberator, my healer, my advocate, my place of perfect security.

And so, tonight I ask You to heal me. I ask You to

remove the memories. To wash them out of my soul. Purge them out of my heart. Eradicate them from every corner of my life until I am free, for I know that You are the God Who frees.

I pray all of this in Jesus's Name. Amen.

A Thought to Carry with Me Today

"Forgiveness brilliantly rewrites the script that we've penned to process the pain and betrayal of our histories. And while such a rewrite does not change history itself, it changes everything about our history."

~ *Craig D. Lounsbrough*

Before this day, I release to God...

___

___

___

___

___

___

___

___

___

___

___

Evening Prayer

Dear God:
Today I believe that You moved in my life. And I believe that not because I felt it, but because I asked for it. I want to be ruled by You, not by my trauma. And I know that to live to the fullest is to be ruled by You to the fullest, for that is the only way to true liberation.

And so I ask that You heal my trauma. Step into my dreams tonight and heal them. Reach into my thoughts tomorrow and rip out every thought that haunts me. Heal my trauma Lord, for You and You alone possess the power to undo what others have done.

I pray all of this in Jesus' Name. Amen.

A Thought to Prepare for Tomorrow

"The darkness that follows a sunset is never so dark that it can change the inevitability of a sunrise."

~ Craig D. Lounsbrough

From this day, I release to God…

Day 25

Wrestling With Fear

"For I am the LORD your God who takes hold of your right hand and says to you, Do not fear; I will help you."

~ Isaiah 41:13

Fear is often less about the thing that we fear, and more about how we've chosen to think about that thing. A natural feature of our fear is the fear of fear. Therefore, when we fear something that fear is often elevated by the fact that we're afraid. Situations themselves typically don't compound our fear. Rather, fear compounds our fear. As such, our level of fear frequently exceeds the actual threat of that which generated our fear in the first place.

Fear feeds on itself more than it feeds off of that which we fear. However, we tend to attribute our level of fear to that which we fear, making that thing, or that event, or that person bigger than whatever it actually is. Our fear is less determined by the reality of the thing that we fear, and more by our fear of fear.

But we might want to ask ourselves some much larger questions. "Why have we chosen fear?" "Why was fear our response?" "How many times is fear our natural response, but it's the wrong response?"

The answers to those questions depend upon how you look at life. Do you look at life as something that happens to you, or something that you make happen? Is your existence determined by everything that surrounds you, or is it determined by the God that surrounds everything that surrounds you? Is your life simply a happenstance existence, or has God assigned you a critical mission that He is determined to see through to completion? How do you look at life, and what impact does your view have on the role that fear will (or will not) play in your life?

"The rains pound and the winds tear and the landscape is shredded under the weight of the storm. Yet the savagery of the storm can never lay a hand on the person whom God has laid His hand upon. Therefore as you live your life, live it in a manner that you never fear the forecast."
~ Craig D. Lounsbrough

Morning Prayer

Dear God:
I am afraid. And often I'm afraid to admit that I'm afraid. I always think that I should be better than that. I should be braver than that. I should be able to confront my fears and send them packing. But I don't.

There are things that I shouldn't fear, but I do. There are people, and situations, and places that I am dreadfully afraid of. Most of this fear is illogical and I know that. But that doesn't change the fact that I'm afraid.

God, you said that You "have not given us a spirit of fear…" Instead You have given us a spirit "of power, and of love, and of a sound mind." That's what I want. I want that kind of power. I want to be bold in You. Strong because of You. Fearless because "You hem me in behind and before, and You lay Your hand upon me." Courageous because You are "my rock, my fortress and my deliverer." I want these things because I no longer want to be hounded by fear.

I pray all of this in Jesus's Name. Amen.

A Thought to Carry with Me Today

"My life is too often driven by the fear of the next moment verses focusing on the privilege that I have the next moment."

~ Craig D. Lounsbrough

Before this day, I release to God...

Evening Prayer

Dear God:
I had my moments of fear today. I didn't like them. I was ashamed of them. I tried to think differently about them or logically tell myself that they weren't as big as I've let them become. But more often than not they got the better of me.

You are the Master of everything, and that includes every fear that I have. You are the Wonderful Counselor. As such, You can counsel me to freedom from fear. You gave your Son the courage to face the brutality of the cross at one of His weakest moments. You can give me the courage to face my fears at my weakest moments as well.

Free me of my fear tonight, tomorrow, and for every tomorrow.

I pray all of this in Jesus' Name. Amen.

A Thought to Prepare for Tomorrow

"What is fear but that 'thing' that we believed to be as powerful as it pretended to be."

~ Craig D. Lounsbrough

From this day, I release to God...

Day 26

Wrestling With Our Faith

"Jesus turned and saw her. 'Take heart, daughter,' he said, 'your faith has healed you.' And the woman was healed at that moment."
~ Matthew 9:22

Faith is a nice concept. A comforting idea. Without a doubt, it would be reassuring to have an unflinching confidence in something that possessed all of the resources necessary to keep us safe in any situation. Yes, that would be nice.

We've all exercised trust in something or someone. However, we often found that faith misplaced, betrayed, possibly idealized, and frequently disappointed. By its very nature, faith embodies a significant level of trust. And when trust exercised in faith is betrayed, the enormity of the betrayal makes faith seem inoperable and impossible.

However, faith is not the issue. The issue is who or what we invested our faith in. The exercise of faith demands the application of wisdom. We cannot exercise faith because it sounds good, or we've been sold on the supposed integrity of some individual, or we've been lulled into embracing some far-flung ideology, or we're simply desperate to believe in something because we don't believe in anything.

Faith only works when it's invested in something or someone who is faithful. It's not that faith doesn't work. It's that faith only works when the thing trusted is what it says it is and will do what it says it will do.

The only thing that meets that criteria in absolute totality is God. Everything else is a faith-failure waiting to happen. God is a faith-builder ready to show you the immense power and relentless comfort that is embodied in exercising faith in Him.

"We have been granted everything that we need to make the world everything that we wish it to be. And it is my ardent prayer that we would likewise be granted faith sufficient to ignite a vision so utterly irrepressible that this 'wish' would become the reality that it is begging to become."

~ Craig D. Lounsbrough

Morning Prayer

Dear God:
The father of the possessed child said to Jesus, "Lord, I believe; help my unbelief!" That is so much of how I feel. I couldn't say it any better than that. At times I believe in spurts, most of which are pretty brief. At other times my belief is a bit more solid. Either, way, I'm asking You to "help my unbelief!"

Lord, sometimes it's the size of the issue that I'm facing. Sometimes it's the nature of the day and whatever mood the day has put me in. It's a person that I fear, or an obligation that I dread. At other times I'm just tired and I find myself not able to believe in much of anything at all.

So, "help my unbelief." Root out within me whatever it is that's standing in the way of the faith that I want to live in and live with. I don't have that kind of faith within me, but I know that's the point. Faith is a gift. Faith is something that I don't have enough of, and so with what little bit of faith I have I'm asking for Your faith to take this tiny bit of mine and blow it wide open. Make me a person of indominable faith. "Help my unbelief" by expanding my belief so that unbelief has no room to not believe.

I pray all of this in Jesus's Name. Amen.

A Thought to Carry with Me Today

"My belief in God was not obtained through some rousing hymns or moving sermon. My faith was burnished hard through pain and trials whose depth was unimaginable and from which recovery seemed impossible. And it was in those most desperate of places that God moved from being a cheerful idea of hymns and sermons to the Master of the unimaginable and the Healer of the impossible."

~ *Craig D. Lounsbrough*

Before this day, I release to God...

____

____

____

____

____

____

Evening Prayer

Dear God:
I want to go to bed every night held fast in a faith that grants me both peace and hope. That's how I want to go to bed every night. But that's also the way that I want to wake up. That's the way that I want to engage the world within me and the world around me.

I want to have the faith that You can give me that kind of faith. And so, my faith is dependent upon You, as is everything else. I want a faith that walks me out beyond all of the places that I stop. I want a faith that challenges me to great things and then prompts me to actually do them. I want a faith that makes every tomorrow bigger than every yesterday. And it is in faith that I ask for that kind of faith.

I pray all of this in Jesus' Name. Amen.

A Thought to Prepare for Tomorrow

"The impossible is always in a desperate search for hands set afire by a heart of faith. For it is the 'fire' ignited by the 'faith' that drives such hands to undertake the task of freeing the impossible to be the possible."

~ *Craig D. Lounsbrough*

From this day, I release to God...

Day 27

Life After Divorce

"Moses permitted you to divorce your wives because your hearts were hard. But it was not this way from the beginning. I tell you that anyone who divorces his wife, except for sexual immorality, and marries another woman commits adultery."
~ Matthew 19:8

"...and the two will become one flesh." In that handful of words there lays an intimacy that the words themselves are entirely unable to encapsulate. Solomon wrote, "A cord of three strands is not quicky broken." Such a beautifully simple sentence highlights the immense power of the marital bond when the couple are united in a mutual relationship with God. Indeed, the bond of marriage is one entirely unparalleled in or by any other relationship.

The potency and power of such a bond explains the immense pain experienced when that bond is broken. It likewise gives insight as to why the impact spills far out beyond the couple and wounds children, parents, relatives, friends, communities, and nations. Marriage is not a convenience. It is a sacred commitment. And when that commitment is violated by the scourge of divorce, generations are rocked.

Yet, divorce happens. It has left multitudes wounded in its wake. The scars are many, the tears beyond counting, and the lives wrecked far too many to reckon. Yet, there is life after divorce. Divorce is the death of a relationship, but it is not the death of you. Life still lays before you. It may look different. The path that you had mapped out may have changed. The dreams might have shifted. But life is still out there.

God has a plan for you. And that plan will never be something that is inferior to the plan that your divorce destroyed. Rather, as a manifold product of His love for you and His genius as exercised on your behalf, that plan can be better than any plan that fell to the death of your marriage.

"I am greatness broken to baseness. And if I gather sufficient courage to actually hear the message of the Gospel, I will embrace my baseness so that God might restore my greatness."

~ Craig D. Lounsbrough

Morning Prayer

Dear God:
I am facing this new day as one person who was once two people. Every morning arrives with a hole in it. Lord, there's a hole in my day before the day even starts. There was a person that had committed to this journey with me. And sadly, I have found that too many commitments are commitments of convenience and ease. These kinds of commitments leave holes. And like so many others that I know, I have one.

But I know that a hole is not an end. It feels that way sometimes, but it's not an end despite how convincing the feeling is. In fact, I know that You have a new beginning for me. You have a beginning that can handily eclipse this ending that seems so dark and so permanent. In the midst of one of their darkest moments, You told Israel, " See, I am doing a new thing! Now it springs up; do you not perceive it? I am making a way in the wilderness and streams in the wasteland." I am praying for that new thing. Make it spring up in my wasteland today.

I pray all of this in Jesus's Name. Amen.

A Thought to Carry with Me Today

"A new start is not about a new day. Rather, it's about a new attitude. And that can happen any day."

~ *Craig D. Lounsbrough*

Before this day, I release to God...

____

____

____

____

____

____

____

____

____

____

____

____

____

____

Evening Prayer

Dear God:
I woke up as one person this morning, and I'm going to bed just the same way. But you are here…today, tomorrow and forever. You said, "I will never leave you nor forsake you." And that commitment is true, reliable, and trustworthy. So I never go to bed alone nor forsaken. Thank You for that.

I don't want to rush out and fill the hole left by my divorce. I know that would be foolish. Rather, I want to grow through this. I want this to make me better, stronger, deeper, and richer as a person in more ways than I thought possible. I refuse to let this beat me. Rather, I pray that it will build me. And so, let's go forward Lord…let's go forward to any and every place that You want to take me.

I pray all of this in Jesus' Name. Amen.

A Thought to Prepare for Tomorrow

"A new day might not necessarily bring new things, but it can bring a new way to do them."

~ Craig D. Lounsbrough

From this day, I release to God...

Day 28

Dealing With Difficult People

"And the Lord's servant must not quarrel; instead, he must be kind to everyone, able to teach, not resentful. Those who oppose him he must gently instruct, in the hope that God will grant them repentance leading them to a knowledge of the truth, and that they will come to their senses and escape from the trap of the devil, who has taken them captive to do his will."

~ 2 Timothy 2:24-26

Difficult people are often a product of the difficulties that they have encountered. In whatever way that they have done it, these individuals have failed to deal with those difficulties. Therefore, they carry these difficulties around inside of them as some sort of internal parasite, spreading them as part of who and what they have become.

This does not excuse the behaviors of these particular people. Rather, it explains them. And if perchance we are one of these people, it explains ourselves to ourselves so that we might find both the insight and motivation to change.

Difficult people are most often hurting people. Their inappropriate and sometimes destructive behaviors are a manifestation of the pain that they carry. Therefore, while their negative behaviors tend to be our focus, we would be wise to look beyond the behaviors to the pain that undergirds the behaviors. We must see the person behind the behaviors or we will doom the person to what they do, not who they are.

And if in fact we can interact with the person rather than respond to their behaviors, we may very well be one of the few who have a chance to help them see who they are and therefore heal from what they've become. And in the life of a hurting person, such an admirable goal would seem worth the risk.

"Always be a bigger person than all of the people who would say that you're not a bigger person. And

while this doesn't necessarily make you bigger,
it will insure that you will never allow
yourself to be smaller."

~ Craig D. Lounsbrough

Morning Prayer

Dear God:
Life is hard enough without people making it harder, because people are very good at doing that. And I confess that sometimes I am those 'people.' I am not immune from allowing the issues within me to trample the people around me.

But You said, "I will give you a new heart and put a new spirit in you; I will remove from you your heart of stone and give you a heart of flesh." And being the difficult person that I can be, I ask this morning that You would do those things in my life today.

And because I can be difficult, help me to be gracious to those who are difficult. Help me to see past their actions to the pain that underlies those actions. Help me to see the wounded hearts, the disappointments, the losses, the self-hatred, and the hopelessness that drives what these people do. And if the opportunity to help them heal is handed to me, give me the wisdom, the discernment, and the determination to help them heal. And in helping them heal, I know that the difficult person in me will heal as well.

I pray all of this in Jesus's Name. Amen.

A Thought to Carry with Me Today

"It's not about being loved by people. It's about loving them enough to do the right thing for them even though they may hate you for it."

~ *Craig D. Lounsbrough*

Before this day, I release to God...

Evening Prayer

Dear God:
I wrestled with the difficult person within me today. And the more that I wrestled with that person, the more I realized how wounded they are. I am difficult because I have not worked to overcome the difficulties within me. And so, I end this day with a commitment to make me different on the inside so that I will be different on the outside.

And help me do the same with the difficult people that I encountered today. I know that I didn't have much grace for them, but I will tomorrow. I know that I allowed their behaviors to raise up some hatred in me, but I will work to love a bit better tomorrow. I know that I no longer wish to be held captive to their behaviors, or to watch them be held captive to them either. And so, tonight, I pray for their healing and freedom.

I pray all of this in Jesus' Name. Amen.

A Thought to Prepare for Tomorrow

"It is far wiser to speak to someone's humanity than to criticize their behaviors."

~ Craig D. Lounsbrough

From this day, I release to God...

Day 29

Dealing With a Physical Handicap

"'Rabbi,' his disciples asked him, 'why was this man born blind? Was it because of his own sins or his parents' sins?' 'It was not because of his sins or his parents' sins,' Jesus answered. 'This happened so the power of God could be seen in him.'"

~ John 9:2-4

We have come to identify a handicap as something that is different from what we presume to be the norm. Whatever this deviation from the norm is, we assume it to be debilitating and somehow diminishing. The overall viability and general life ability of the person with the handicap is viewed as reduced and marginalized.

These definitions are inherently confining and minimizing. They assume a handicap as entirely diminishing. What is missed in such a constricting view is the gift in the handicap. The handicap forces adjustments. It demands a different way to engage life. It creates a unique and important perspective not shared by many. A handicap cants one's view of self, of others, of life, of reality, of possibilities, and more.

This differing view comes with unique outlooks on life that open up opportunities and possibilities that had never been considered before. It presents the world with imaginative ideas, a renewed appreciation of life, a fresh sense of what's important and what's not, as well as a grid that quickly screens out the unnecessary things in life that so many of us errantly view as necessary.

In essence, there is a priceless gift in every handicap. That doesn't make the handicap easy. But it does make it priceless. And just maybe it is the accumulation of our handicaps and the rich lessons within them that makes us great if we only take the time to pay attention to them.

"Once I realize that my greatest resources are cleverly hidden in the disguise of my many handicaps, I have finally discovered the resources that I thought could only be found in my greatest strengths."

~ Craig D. Lounsbrough

Morning Prayer

Dear God:
I have my handicaps. Some are obvious. Some are not. Many I am in denial of. Most I hate. Regardless, I have my handicaps. And I have chosen to see them as liabilities that I have been unfairly and cruelly burdened with. I have spent my life trying to cover them up or work around them. And neither of those approaches have worked.

Jesus disciples asked him why a man had been born blind. And Jesus said, "this happened so that the works of God might be displayed in him." I don't look at my handicap that way. I don't see it as an opportunity for God to display His works through this thing that I carry. I see it as a curse. As an injustice perpetrated upon me. I hate it.

But I pray that You would work through my handicap. That You would be seen through this thing that haunts me. That You would use what I despise to work out in my life whatever it is that You want to work out. Help me to realize that not having this handicap would rob You of the opportunity to show Yourself through my life in order to change the lives around me. And to miss that might be the biggest handicap of all.

I pray all of this in Jesus's Name. Amen.

A Thought to Carry with Me Today

"I will most certainly focus on one of two things; the nagging deficits of my handicap, or the masterful honing brought about by my handicap. And my choice of focus will determine if my handicap will remain a handicap."

~ Craig D. Lounsbrough

Before this day, I release to God...

Evening Prayer

Dear God:
I'm still not certain that I know what to do with my handicap. I'm trying to see it as a platform that You can use to show people who You are and what You can do. I'm not certain how that all works, but I'm pretty certain that it can work.

And so, help me to see the assets in my handicap. Help me to change how I see this thing that the world labels as disability. Help me to understand that every disability is a possibility that's waiting to be utilized and unleashed.

Tonight I give my handicap to You to be used in whatever way You wish to use it. Help people see You in ways that they would otherwise miss. Save lives. Change families. Grant hope. Give perspective. Heal communities. Transform nations through the handicap that I now give to You.

I pray all of this in Jesus' Name. Amen.

A Thought to Prepare for Tomorrow

"Without a doubt, the most ingenious plan I could ever hope to devise would be to trade my plans for God's."

~ Craig Lounsbrough

From this day, I release to God...

Day 30

Healing From Sexual Abuse

"When you pass through the waters, I will be with you; and when you pass through the rivers, they will not sweep over you. When you walk through the fire, you will not be burned; the flames will not set you ablaze. For I am the LORD your God,"

~ Psalm 43:2-3a

At times our humanity is ignored. We become the objects of those who seek to meet their needs in some destructive and entirely careless manner. We are relegated to a commodity to be used and then discarded at the pleasure of the one doing the using and the discarding.

This strips us of our uniqueness and our value. We are an item that is not even accorded any respect as an item. Our lives are to be bartered away in the service of those who are willing to fulfill their own desires at the destruction of another.

Such is the nature of sexual abuse. It is a violation that is never held to the particular moment within which it transpires. It is a violation of every moment for the rest of the victim's life. It carries with it a scar that cuts across the person's entire life. Nothing is left untouched or unsoiled.

There is a desperation to sexual abuse. There's no place to run. No hiding. No hole deep enough to bury the shame, no words potent enough to restore a shattered self-image, and no means by which to erase a now indelible history.

Yet, God heals all wounds. As Isaiah declared, "…by His stripes we are healed." Your wounds are not your prison. Your scars are not a commentary of who you are, or who you will be. None of these are your story. By His stripes yours are healed. You are His story. Amazing, beautiful and true.

"Your story is not written by those who abused the opportunities that they had to pen a line or two on the pages of your life. For your story is written by the God whose story will erase all of the lesser lines of men."

~ *Craig D. Lounsbrough*

Morning Prayer

Dear God:
There are some sacred things in life that should never be violated. And when they are, everything suddenly becomes different. Everything becomes dark. The ability to trust vanishes. We are consumed with shame. And we feel that we are damaged goods. I have felt these things more than once.

What do I do with a history that I can't change, but also can't forget? What do I do with emotions that won't give me a break? What do I do with all of the stuff that is now part of my life because of the actions of someone else?

Dear God, the Bible says that You, "heal the brokenhearted and bind up their wounds." Without a doubt, I am brokenhearted and wounded…so much so that I don't see a way to recover. But You are the Master of recovery. You heal what no one can. You bind up our wounds and You tell us that these wounds are not forever. You've said that every wound is an opportunity that we simply can't see as an opportunity. So, take my wounds and in whatever way You do that, make them beautiful. Make them what I never thought that they could be. Make them Your opportunity.

I pray all of this in Jesus's Name. Amen.

A Thought to Carry with Me Today

"Pain is the thing that I am most desperate to avoid,
yet if I have any hope to grow it is the thing
that I most desperately need."

~ *Craig D. Lounsbrough*

Before this day, I release to God...

____

____

____

____

____

____

____

____

____

____

____

Evening Prayer

Dear God:
I'm going to bed knowing that the nightmares are just a moment away. But I don't have to sleep to have nightmares because the memories that I have when I'm awake are just as horrifying. I am haunted by the memories that are often worse than the actual moment of abuse.

I am asking You to heal me from that which I cannot heal myself. I am helpless before the memories, and the trauma, and the fear that is always chasing me. Dear God, please do for me what I cannot do for myself. Rid me of the pain. Press the shame right out of my soul. Tell me that I have the value that I can't see. Strip the memories of the darkness that always comes with them. Grant me a peace that I don't even remember but wish to remember yet again.

I pray all of this in Jesus' Name. Amen.

A Thought to Prepare for Tomorrow

"I might have my holes, but the healing of today means that they will be smaller in every tomorrow, including the one that is now only hours away."

~ Craig D. Lounsbrough

From this day, I release to God...

Conclusion

I prayed through the writing of this book, much like I've prayed through the living of my life. It is no easy task to write a book on prayer. In writing such a book, one could easily fall prey to simplistic ideas, warm notions, and inspiring thoughts.

However, prayer must have a honed and instinctual relevancy that intersects the deepest pain, the most impenetrable darkness, catastrophic losses of unimaginable proportions, and horrors of the most horrific kind. It must have a reach that confidently exceeds anything that life can bring against us. By its very nature it must possess a resiliency and a power that leaves it standing when everything that we prayed over has fallen in its battle against us or been healed because of that battle. If prayer does not possess these things, how then is it relevant?

More than once my life has been intersected by pain and loss that I could not have imagined. At several dark seasons in my own journey my life has been stripped bare and beaten to a pulp, leaving me with little to somehow begin again. I don't claim to know the worst of pain. But I know enough to shape the way that I pray about pain. And that prayer must be more than simplistic ideas, warm notions, and inspiring thoughts.

This book then was written to be more than all of that. It was written with the realities of life clearly in mind and the promises of God at the forefront of my mind. It was written for the real world with a steady eye focused on a real God that stands ready to overcome that world. It is my hope that crafting this book in just such a manner as this has provided you an effective and meaningful means by which to pray with certainty and power in the midst of your real world. May this book shape and empower your prayer life in a manner robust, life-altering and life-liberating. That is my prayer for you.